WHAT'S THE POINT OF
SCIENCE?

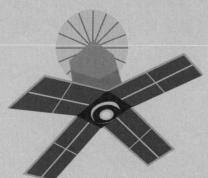

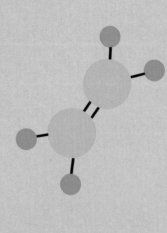

DK | Penguin Random House

Senior Editor Steven Carton
Project Art Editor Joe Lawrence
Illustrator Clarisse Hassan
Editors Edward Aves, Ben Morgan
Designers Samantha Richiardi, Lauren Quinn
Writers Edward Aves, Ben Ffrancon Davies, A. M. Dassu
Historical Consultant Philip Parker
UK Media Archive Romaine Werblow
Managing Editor Rachel Fox
Managing Art Editor Owen Peyton Jones
Production Controller Laura Andrews
Production Editor Gillian Reid
Jacket Designer Akiko Kato
Jacket Design Development Manager Sophia MTT

First published in Great Britain in 2021 by
Dorling Kindersley Limited
DK, One Embassy Gardens, 8 Viaduct Gardens,
London, SW11 7BW

The authorized representative in the EEA is
Dorling Kindersley Verlag GmbH. Arnulfstr. 124,
80636 Munich, Germany

Copyright © 2021 Dorling Kindersley Limited
A Penguin Random House Company
10 9 8 7 6 5 4 3 2 1
001–314329–Oct/2021

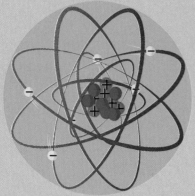
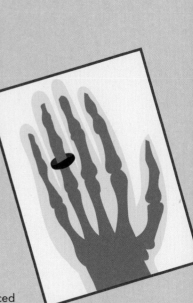

A CIP catalogue record for this book
is available from the British Library.
ISBN: 978-0-2413-8184-7

Printed and bound in China

For the curious
www.dk.com

MIX
Paper from
responsible sources
FSC™ C018179

This book was made with Forest Stewardship
Council™ certified paper – one small step
in DK's commitment to a sustainable future.
For more information go to
www.dk.com/our-green-pledge

WHAT'S THE POINT OF
SCIENCE?

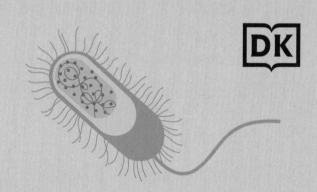

DK

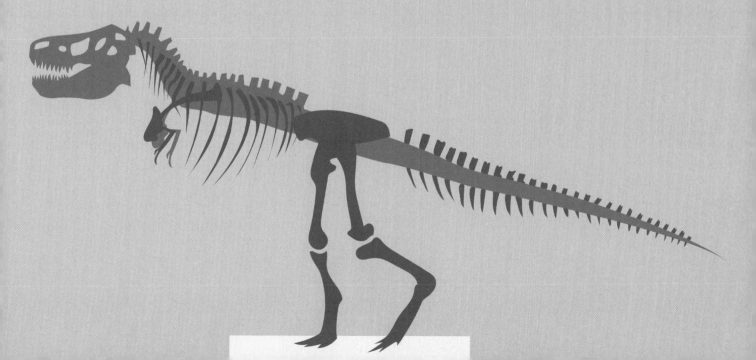

CONTENTS

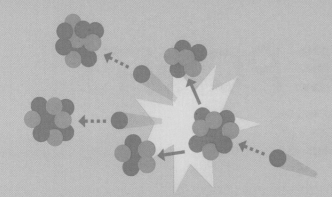

Some dates have BCE and CE after them. These are short for "before the Common Era" and "Common Era". The Common Era dates from when people think Jesus was born. Where the exact date of an event is not known, "c." is used. This is short for the Latin word *circa*, meaning "around", and indicates that the date is approximate.

WHAT'S THE POINT OF SCIENCE?

Look around you – science is everywhere, from the tiniest gadget to everything we know about the Universe! Scientists are people who are always asking questions, always trying to know more about the world around us in order to improve that world and our lives in it. Their hard work and endless curiosity have given us many things – here are just a few.

DINOSAURS!

Everyone loves dinosaurs, but without paleontologists and biologists we would know very little about them and other prehistoric life. By finding, carefully extracting, and preserving fossils, these experts have reconstructed the time of the dinosaurs, and also the eras before and after.

MAKING YOU BETTER

Doctors, dentists, physiotherapists, psychologists, and more all rely on science to figure out what is wrong with us, and then how to make us better. Science also helps to improve these treatments to make recovery even more likely in future.

CARING FOR EARTH

Scientists have made us aware of how we are harming our home planet. Many hope that scientists across the planet can work together to find an answer to global warming and help to save life on Earth.

BRICK BY BRICK

Our knowledge of forces and materials from physics has meant that we can build ever more impressive and beautiful buildings. We all need places to work and learn in, have fun in, and live in – science helps architects and engineers figure out a way to make these places become reality.

EXPLORING THE UNIVERSE

Everything we know about space and the Universe has come from scientists making observations and collecting information. In recent decades, they have launched giant rockets to get spacecraft off Earth and into the Solar System to collect even more knowledge.

KEEPING YOU SAFE

For much of human history, preventable viruses, diseases, and infections have cut short the lives of millions of people across the world. With vaccines, antibiotics, and other drugs, scientists and doctors have managed to save countless people and vastly increase health and wellbeing, too.

HOME COMFORTS

From the clothes you wear, to exercise equipment, and even this very book, science has had a huge role in creating new materials that make the things that we enjoy, learn from, and give us peace in our daily lives.

EXPLORING EARTH

Whether we're talking about explorers voyaging around the world hundreds of years ago, or tourists getting on an aeroplane to travel to a different country today, science has unlocked many breakthroughs that make travel and exploration safer, more comfortable, and more exciting.

FUN STUFF

Want to have some fun? Science has you covered! Everything from fireworks, to electronic musical instruments, to video games consoles have happened due to amazing scientific breakthroughs.

UNDERSTANDING OURSELVES

Why do we look the way we do? What goes on inside our bodies? How do animals survive and change over time? Science has given us answers to these questions and more, and will continue to answer questions we will have in the future, too.

PREDICTING THE WEATHER

There might be Sun or there might be a storm – either way, scientists can let us know by gathering data on the weather and explaining what it all means. Weather forecasting is especially important to farmers, pilots, and sailors, who need to know what the weather will be to be able to do their jobs.

FOOD FOR ALL

With more and more people in the world, growing nutrient-rich food is more important now than ever. Our understanding of biology and chemistry enhances our ability to make the most of Earth and its resources.

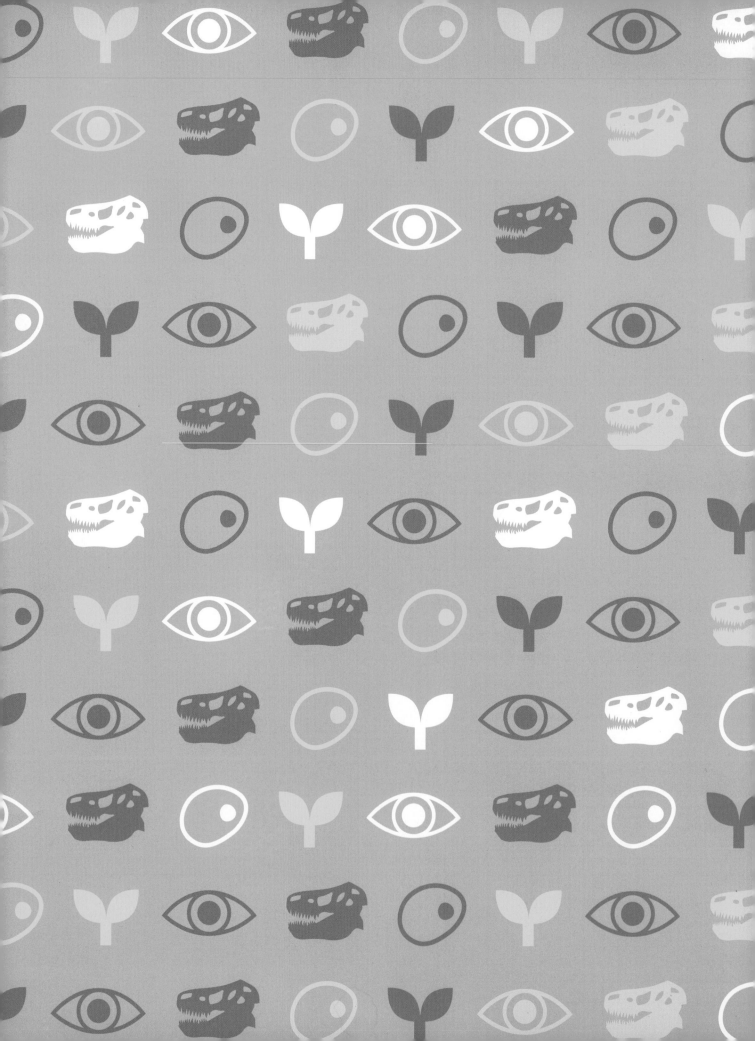

WHAT'S THE POINT OF
BIOLOGY?

Have you ever wondered how we fight terrible viruses and infections?
Or what makes people look different from one another? Or how animals
hunt their prey? All these questions, and millions of others, can be
answered by studying biology – the study of life in all its forms:
from tiny, single-celled bacteria to large, complex animals like us.

WHY DO WE NEED BIOLOGY?

If it's alive, biology is involved somehow, because biology is the study of life. If you've ever wondered why we need sleep, or why animals behave the way they do, or what is needed to make the food we eat every day, then biology is the first place to go to find answers to all of these questions, and more!

EVERYDAY BIOLOGY

Scientists who study biology are called biologists. They study everything from how the cells inside our body work to how huge herds of animals adapt to their environment and rely on each other to survive. Biologists are often the first to alert us about dangerous illnesses or if an animal population is under threat from human actions.

Precious plants
Without plants, there would be no life on Earth. Plants use the Sun's energy to make their own food, and are eaten as food by animals and humans. Humans also can make materials from some plants, and sometimes burn them to provide heat.

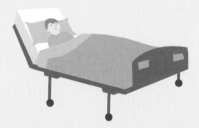

Biologists study how the human body reacts to diseases and infections, and use that information to develop cures.

Animal behaviour is a huge part of biology – including how animals feed, play, reproduce, and rest.

Biologists study how living things interact with their environment, and how to protect endangered animals, such as orangutans.

Biologists help us to understand the importance of exercise, sleep, and how to have a balanced diet to keep our bodies and minds healthy.

Agricultural scientists study the best ways to grow healthy crops, such as bananas, and rear animals for food.

WHAT IS BIOLOGY?

From the ingredients needed for life to happen, to how humans, animals, plants, and even single-celled organisms live, grow, reproduce, and die, biology is the science that seeks to explain the living world.

Trees use sunlight to make their own food through a process called photosynthesis.

Biologists study how our brains work, including how we respond to things we like, such as rest and music.

Much of how you are, from your height to even your personality, is decided by your biology.

Bees display a range of unique behaviour, from how they organize their hives to how they find food.

Biologists have shown that birds are the closest living relatives to the dinosaurs.

WHAT'S THE POINT OF CELLS?

Just like a building is made up of bricks, all living things – from tiny bacteria to fully grown human beings – are made up of cells. Cells cannot be seen without a microscope. Not all cells are the same: plant cells have rigid cell walls to protect the cell and give them structure, and there are different types of animal cell, all doing specific jobs.

Chloroplasts use energy from sunlight for the cell to make its food.

Plant cell

Plant cells have spaces called vacuoles to store food, water, and waste.

In both animal and plant cells, mitochondria turn food into energy.

Plant cells have a rigid cell wall, which keeps the cell's shape.

Ribosomes make protein.

The cell nucleus in animal and plant cells stores genetic information.

The cytoplasm is a jelly-like liquid inside the cell.

Animal cell

CAN YOU SEE THE PAST?

When something dies, in the right circumstances it can sometimes leave behind a fossil – an impression of its body preserved for millions of years in rock. Fossil hunter Mary Anning scoured the cliffs at Lyme Regis in England, UK, for fossils to sell to collectors, but her groundbreaking finds would end up revolutionizing the way scientists thought about the history of life on Earth.

1 As children, Mary and her brother Joseph helped their father to collect fossilized ammonite and belemnite shells. The family made their living by selling these so-called "curiosities" to collectors – nobody really knew for sure what they were.

2 In 1811, Mary – then aged 12 – and Joseph discovered a fossilized skull, unlike anything they'd ever found before. Mary later carefully uncovered the rest of the fossil, a 5-m- (16-ft-) long skeleton. She had unearthed the very first complete fossil of an *Ichthyosaurus*, a mysterious animal.

Ichthyosaurus means "fish lizard".

Belemnite

Ammonite

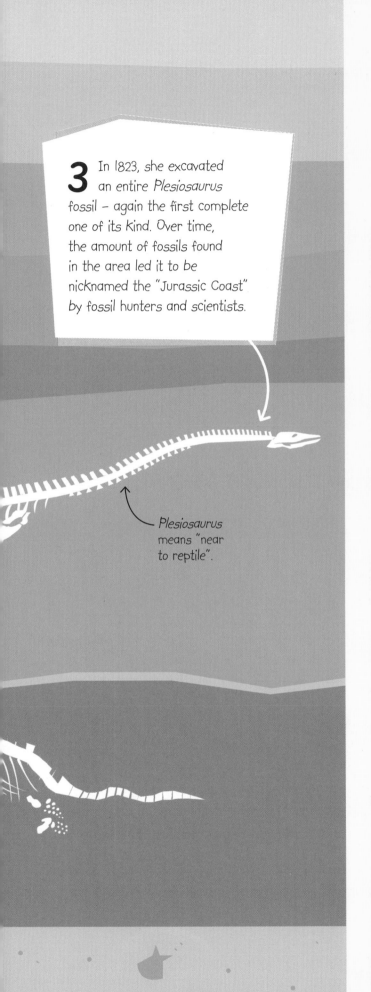

3 In 1823, she excavated an entire *Plesiosaurus* fossil – again the first complete one of its kind. Over time, the amount of fossils found in the area led it to be nicknamed the "Jurassic Coast" by fossil hunters and scientists.

Plesiosaurus means "near to reptile".

Understanding the science
LAYERS OF THE PAST

Anning's work contributed greatly to our understanding of prehistoric animals, and how to identify and date them. We now know that the deeper a fossil is in a section of rock, the older it is. Below is part of the geological timeline of Earth, which is measured in million years ago (MYA).

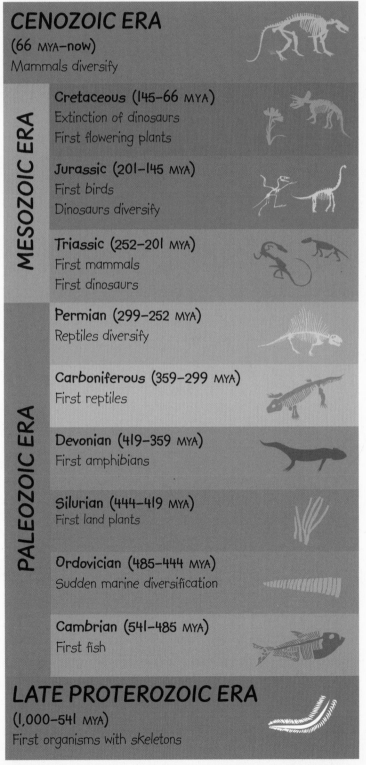

CENOZOIC ERA
(66 MYA–now)
Mammals diversify

MESOZOIC ERA

Cretaceous (145–66 MYA)
Extinction of dinosaurs
First flowering plants

Jurassic (201–145 MYA)
First birds
Dinosaurs diversify

Triassic (252–201 MYA)
First mammals
First dinosaurs

PALEOZOIC ERA

Permian (299–252 MYA)
Reptiles diversify

Carboniferous (359–299 MYA)
First reptiles

Devonian (419–359 MYA)
First amphibians

Silurian (444–419 MYA)
First land plants

Ordovician (485–444 MYA)
Sudden marine diversification

Cambrian (541–485 MYA)
First fish

LATE PROTEROZOIC ERA
(1,000–541 MYA)
First organisms with skeletons

HOW DO FOSSILS FORM?

Not everything that dies becomes a fossil. In fact, it's a rare process that takes a very long time. The conditions have to be just right for something to leave behind an imprint in rock, which then may be found and carefully unearthed millions of years later.

The animal dies.

Fossils are only found in sedimentary rock.

The bones and teeth of the animal are all that remain.

1 When an animal dies, it can only become a fossil if it is buried quickly by something like sand or mud, which makes the carcass decay more slowly.

2 The animal's soft tissue – such as its skin and muscles – decays to reveal its skeleton, which gets covered with little bits of rock and minerals called sediment. Over time, these particles of rock build up and compact to form sedimentary rock.

REAL WORLD

Dino feathers
Scientists used to think all dinosaurs were scaly, like crocodiles and lizards, but we now know that some of them had feathers. Dinosaur feathers have been found preserved in fossilized tree resin, or "amber", as in this example found in 2016.

DID YOU KNOW?

Fossil poo!
Not all fossils are dinosaurs, or even animals. Plants, eggs, and even footprints can become fossils, too. Scientists have also found fossilized poo, which is known as a "coprolite".

The skeleton has become a fossil.

Great care is taken when unearthing the fossil to protect it from damage.

3 Water within the rock soaks into the bones and eventually dissolves them. When this water drains away, it leaves behind minerals that create an imprint of the skeleton in the rock.

4 Over time, some rock and earth wears away due to erosion, and older rock moves up from the depths in a process called uplift. This brings some fossils closer to the surface, where they can potentially be found by paleontologists.

LASTING IMPACT

The fossils found by Mary Anning and other paleontologists have completely changed our understanding of Earth's history. Fossils let us look back in time, millions of years before humans existed. Incredible ancient fossils provide concrete evidence for the theory of evolution, inspire people to learn about our planet's history, and spur scientists on to find out even more about life on prehistoric Earth.

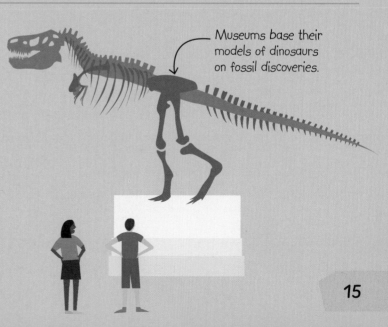

Museums base their models of dinosaurs on fossil discoveries.

HOW TO STOP A VIRUS

For much of history, diseases spread by microbes (harmful microorganisms) killed almost half of all people. One of the biggest killers was smallpox, which was caused by a virus that spread in people's breath. Smallpox killed and blinded millions, but in 1796 an English doctor found a way of safely preventing it: vaccination. By 1980, smallpox was completely eradicated.

1 Around 500 years ago in China, people realized that a mild case of smallpox may protect you from the full disease. Doctors blew smallpox scabs up people's noses to infect them. It sometimes worked, but many people got the full disease and died.

2 By the 1700s, doctors in Europe had found a slightly less deadly way of preventing smallpox: they used smallpox scabs to infect a person's skin. Russian empress Catherine the Great had the treatment. She felt sick for two weeks but it worked.

Pus and scabs from smallpox victims were rubbed into a scratch.

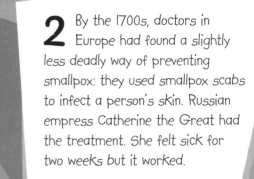

3 In the late 1700s, the English doctor Edward Jenner noticed that milkmaids didn't get smallpox. He wondered if this was because cows had infected them with cowpox – a similar but much less dangerous disease.

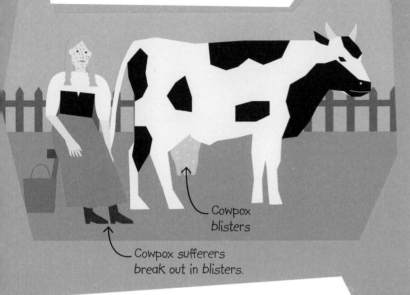

Cowpox blisters

Cowpox sufferers break out in blisters.

4 In 1796, Jenner took pus from a milkmaid's cowpox blisters and rubbed it into a cut on a boy's arm. Later, Jenner injected the boy with smallpox, but he didn't get sick – he was immune. The treatment became known as a vaccine, after the Latin word *vacca* which means "cow".

Jenner rubbed cowpox germs into the arm of James Phipps, an eight-year-old boy.

Understanding the science
HOW VIRUSES WORK

Viruses are the tiniest microbes and cause many different diseases, from common colds and chickenpox to rabies and COVID-19. They reproduce by hijacking our cells and making them manufacture new copies of themselves.

Invading cold virus

After invading a person's body, a virus uses molecules called antigens on its surface to find the right kind of cell and stick to it.

Throat cell

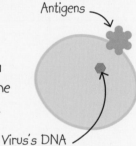

Antigens

The virus injects its genes into the cell as a molecule of DNA (or the related molecule RNA).

Virus's DNA

New viral DNA

The virus's genes take over the cell. They force it to start manufacturing copies of the virus's antigens and genes.

New antigens

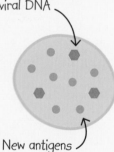

Cell bursts

The cell assembles these parts into hundreds of copies of the invading virus. They burst out of the cell, destroying it, to find new cells to invade.

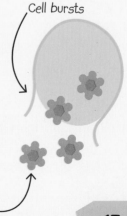

Copies of the original virus

HOW VACCINES WORK

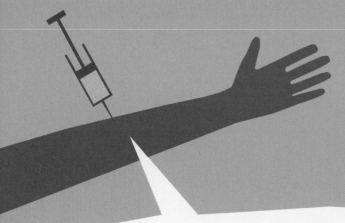

Vaccines work by stimulating your body's immune system. Your immune system continually hunts for new germs, which it attacks with chemicals called antibodies. When this happens, your immune system also creates "memory cells" that remember the invader. If the same germ tries to infect you again, memory cells launch an attack so swift that the germ is destroyed before it makes you ill – you have become immune.

1 Most vaccines are made from modified germs and have the same antigen molecules on their surface as those germs. When a vaccine or germ enters the body, white blood cells try to lock on to its antigens using antibody molecules. They try thousands of different types of antibody. Eventually a match is found.

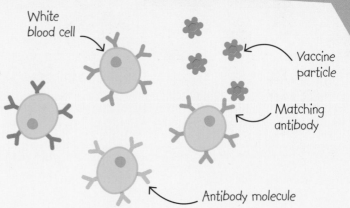

White blood cell

Vaccine particle

Matching antibody

Antibody molecule

2 Triggered by the match, the successful white blood cell divides to make millions of new cells, all with the matching antibody molecules. The new cells release the antibodies in huge amounts. The antibodies travel through the body and stick to germs. They act as beacons for cells called phagocytes, which swallow and kill the germs.

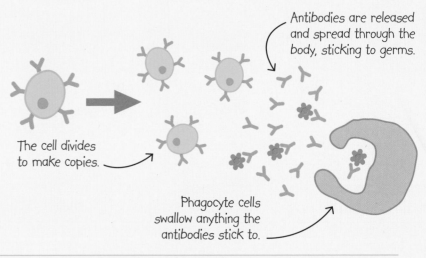

The cell divides to make copies.

Antibodies are released and spread through the body, sticking to germs.

Phagocyte cells swallow anything the antibodies stick to.

3 The successful white blood cell also makes memory cells. These stay in the body for years, ready to mount a faster attack if the germ returns. The memory cells give the body immunity.

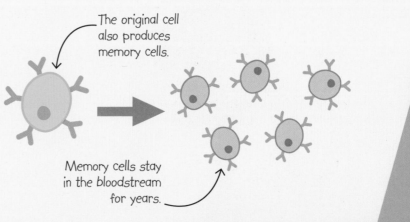

The original cell also produces memory cells.

Memory cells stay in the bloodstream for years.

Virus mutations

Viruses such as influenza can evolve quickly due to mutations – changes in their genes. If a mutation changes the shape of a virus's antigens, the antibodies in a person's body may no longer recognize it, which means the person is no longer immune. This is why the same person can get influenza (flu) year after year.

COVID-19 pandemic

In December 2019, the World Health Organization learned of a deadly new lung disease in Wuhan, China. The COVID-19 pandemic swept across the world and killed millions. Within a year, scientists developed at least three effective vaccines to prevent the disease, but the virus may never fully go away because of mutations.

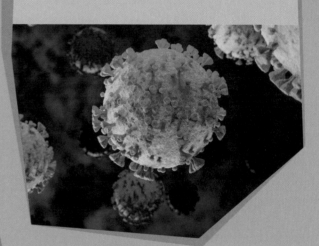

Measles
530,217 cases

Smallpox
29,005 cases

Polio
16,316 cases

WHY DO VACCINES MATTER?

Vaccines save millions of people every year. The measles vaccine alone is estimated to have prevented the deaths of 20 million children worldwide from 2000 to 2016. Although very few diseases have been totally eradicated by vaccines, many diseases that were once common are now very rare.

Mumps
162,344 cases

Rubella
47,745 cases

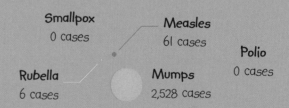

Smallpox
0 cases

Measles
61 cases

Polio
0 cases

Rubella
6 cases

Mumps
2,528 cases

Annual US disease
cases in 1910

Annual US disease
cases in 2010

19

1 For thousands of years, people had been influencing genes without knowing it by selectively breeding animals and plants. This involves allowing useful traits to make it to the next generation, and stopping bad traits from being passed on.

2 Gregor Mendel started studying how traits are passed on in the 1850s. He began by experimenting with peas in his monastery's garden. He chose peas because they grow quickly, make many seeds, have clearly different traits, and can be bred in a simple, controlled environment, making it easier to discover how they pass on their characteristics.

Wild wolves were selectively bred over many generations to become friendly dogs.

Mendel cross-fertilized the plants himself by rubbing pollen from the male part of one plant onto the female part of another.

WHY DO I LOOK LIKE ME?

There is a reason why you often look like your family, and that reason is genes – inherited traits that you get from your parents. The study of how traits are passed from one generation to the next is called genetics. We've long known about genetics, but it took the experiments of a Czech-born monk to explain just how it works.

3 Over the course of eight years, Mendel grew about 29,000 pea plants. He looked at specific traits, such as the colour of the pods, peas, and flowers, across many generations. He discovered that there was no "blending" of traits – for example, crossing pea plants with purple flowers with those that had white flowers did not lead to a light purple flower.

Pea plants can be tall or short.

Flowers can *be* white or purple, and they can *be* on the end of the stem or along its length.

Pea pods can *be* green or yellow, and the peas within them can *be* green or yellow, too.

When Mendel cross-fertilized plants that had always had green pods with those that had always had yellow pods, the next generation always had green pods.

When those green-pod plants were cross-fertilized with each other, they produced green and yellow pods in a ratio of 3:1.

First generation

Second generation

4 Mendel discovered that certain characteristics of the pea plants changed from generation to generation, with some traits skipping a generation and some appearing more commonly than others. He reasoned that certain traits are dominant – which means that they are more likely to be the ones shown in the offspring plant.

HOW GENES WORK

Mendel reasoned that each parent has two versions of every trait, and each parent gives one version of a trait to each offspring. Some versions of traits (such as green pods) were dominant over others (such as the yellow pods), which are recessive. We now call these traits "genes", and the different versions of each trait "alleles".

Each parent has two alleles for each trait. If the trait is dominant, such as green pods, it is capitalized.

The Punnett square is used to show allele combinations and how they look in the offspring plants.

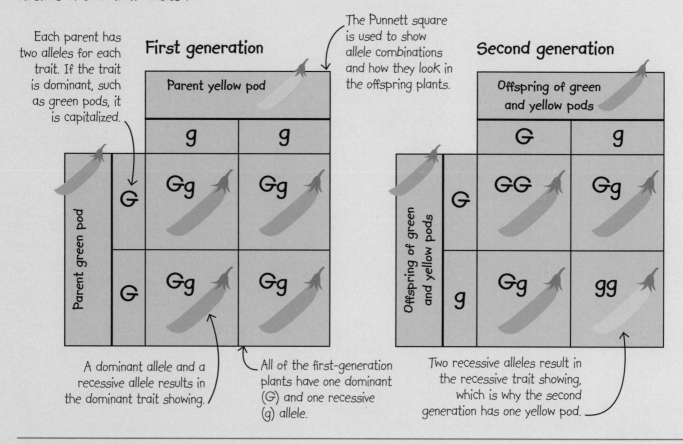

First generation

Parent yellow pod

	g	g
G	Gg	Gg
G	Gg	Gg

Parent green pod

Second generation

Offspring of green and yellow pods

	G	g
G	GG	Gg
g	Gg	gg

Offspring of green and yellow pods

A dominant allele and a recessive allele results in the dominant trait showing.

All of the first-generation plants have one dominant (G) and one recessive (g) allele.

Two recessive alleles result in the recessive trait showing, which is why the second generation has one yellow pod.

BEING SELECTIVE

We now use our knowledge of genes to improve our ability to selectively breed things with desirable traits. Breeders select two parents that have the traits they want more of. For example, we use selective breeding to develop sheep that can produce more wool, and for crops to be more abundant. We can also selectively breed animals and plants to have greater resistance to pests and disease. All of these have a huge impact on how much food we can produce.

Disease resistance in both plants and animals increases food production.

Animals are also selectively bred to be bigger, so they produce more meat.

Crops like wheat are selectively bred to be healthier, tastier, and more bountiful.

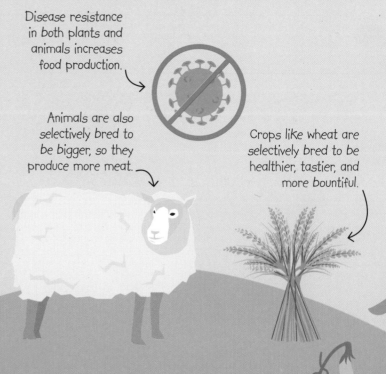

SIMILARITIES AND DIFFERENCES

Genetics in humans is complex and not as simple to predict as it is in pea plants. This is because each of our characteristics is usually controlled by more than one gene, and, as we have seen, certain traits might skip a generation only to appear in the next one. The best we can do for certain traits, such as the eye colour of a child, is to make rough predictions based on the traits that the parents have.

Parent 1	Parent 2	Child eye colour chance		
+	=	75%	18.75%	6.25%
+	=	50%	37.5%	12.5%
+	=	50%	0%	50%
+	=	<1%	75%	25%
+	=	0%	50%	50%
+	=	0%	1%	99%

REAL WORLD

Genetic fingerprinting

Everyone's genes are different, which means that they can be used to identify us, just like a fingerprint. Police use genetic science to analyse hair or saliva left at a crime scene to work out who the criminal is.

If one parent has brown eyes, and one has blue eyes, there is an equal chance the child will have brown or blue eyes.

Also, little mistakes can sometimes happen when a parent's alleles are copied for their children, leading to differences. This is why some people don't look like either of their parents, or they have a particular trait – such as tallness – that their parents don't have. These differences become part of their genetic information, which they can pass on if they have kids in future.

The daughter's height genes are clearly different from those of her parents.

HOW TO SAVE MILLIONS OF LIVES

During World War I, millions of soldiers died – but not all because they were killed in battle. Many died because their wounds had become infected by microscopic organisms called bacteria. For thousands of years, bacteria had made even small wounds deadly, but all that changed thanks to a discovery made completely by chance!

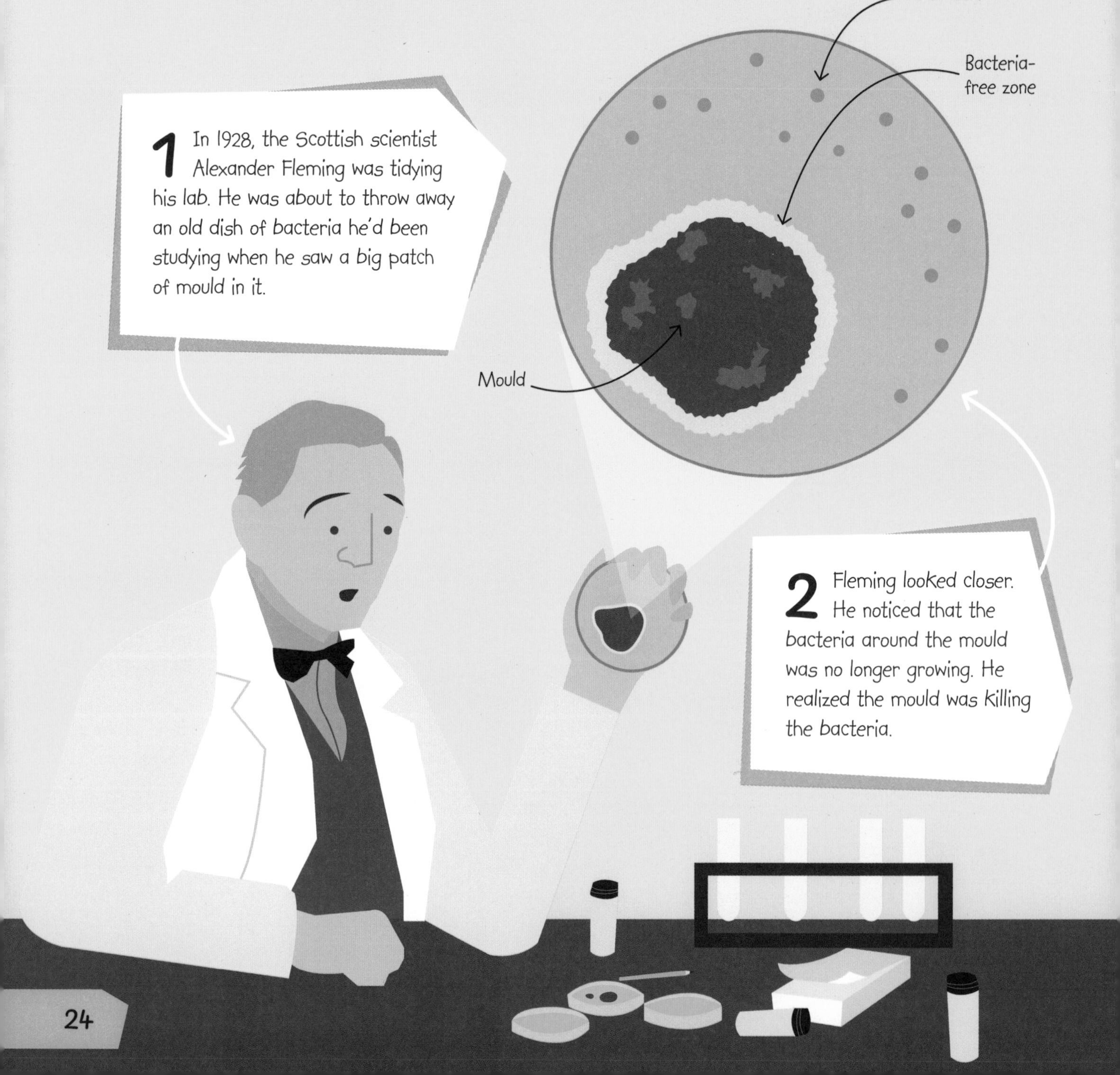

Bacteria

Bacteria-free zone

1 In 1928, the Scottish scientist Alexander Fleming was tidying his lab. He was about to throw away an old dish of bacteria he'd been studying when he saw a big patch of mould in it.

Mould

2 Fleming looked closer. He noticed that the bacteria around the mould was no longer growing. He realized the mould was killing the bacteria.

3 Fleming realized he might have chanced upon a weapon to fight bacteria. He set his lab team to work. After a few weeks, they identified the fungus that had killed the bacteria, and Fleming named it penicillin. He had discovered antibiotics – bacteria killers.

4 For the fungus to be made into an effective medicine, it needed to be purified and produced in bulk, which proved very difficult. Twelve years later, a team of scientists at Oxford University, UK, produced an injectable medicine.

5 By now, World War II had broken out, and an effective antibiotic was needed more than ever. The Oxford scientists persuaded drug companies in the US to support more research and produce antibiotics in bulk. By 1944, millions of doses had been manufactured to help the war effort.

WHAT ARE BACTERIA?

Bacteria are tiny single-celled organisms that are found everywhere on Earth. A teaspoon of soil contains at least 100 million bacteria, and your body contains about 40 trillion. Some are helpful, such as the ones in your intestines that help you digest food, but others can cause deadly diseases. Bacteria are usually divided into three groups, according to their shape.

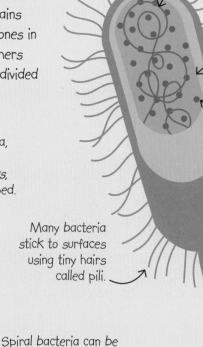

Inside a bacterium cell, the genes that help it to reproduce are stored in a tangled loop of DNA.

The DNA floats in a thick gel called cytoplasm.

Ribosomes make the proteins the bacterium needs.

A strong cell wall surrounds the cytoplasm.

Many bacteria stick to surfaces using tiny hairs called pili.

Some bacteria move using a flagellum, a kind of tail.

Cocci bacteria, such as *Streptococcus*, are ball-shaped.

Bacilli are rod-shaped.

Bacillus

Streptococcus

Spirochaete

Spirillum

Vibrio

Spiral bacteria can be comma-shaped (*Vibrio*), or have spirals that may be thick (*Spirillum*) or thin and corkscrew-like (spirochaete).

HOW PENICILLIN WORKS

Since World War II, penicillin antibiotics have been used to treat millions of patients suffering from bacterial infections. *Streptococcus* is a type of bacteria that lives in the throats of humans and animals. Normally it doesn't cause any problems, but for people with weakened immunity, it can move down to the lungs, where it may cause a dangerous inflammation called pneumonia.

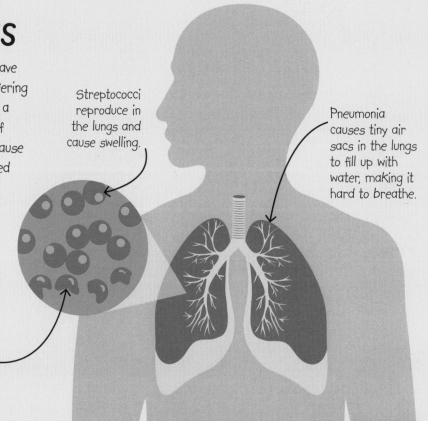

Streptococci reproduce in the lungs and cause swelling.

Pneumonia causes tiny air sacs in the lungs to fill up with water, making it hard to breathe.

Antibiotics fight the bacteria by weakening their strong cell walls. Eventually the cell walls burst, causing the bacteria to die.

SUPERBUGS

Antibiotics have saved many millions of lives, but scientists soon discovered a problem. The bacteria we fight with antibiotics are continually changing thanks to mutations in their genes. Some mutations make them resistant to antibiotics, and the more we use antibiotics, the more common these resistant bacteria become. These highly resistant, dangerous bacteria are known as superbugs.

Non-resistant bacteria

Because of natural selection, the resistant bacterium survives while the rest die.

A bacterium mutates, and becomes resistant to antibiotics.

The resistant bacteria multiply, and eventually they are all resistant to antibiotics.

Tough bacterium

Bacteria are so hardy that they can even live in the extreme cold and radiation levels experienced in space. Scientists placed some of the bacterium *Deinococcus radiodurans* on the outside of the International Space Station. It survived for three years, which may mean that some life does not need Earth's environment to survive.

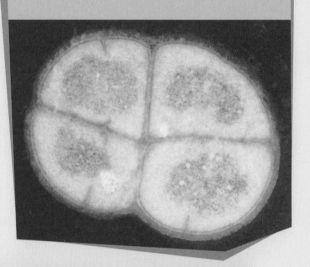

GLOW IN THE DARK

Some living things use bacteria to make their own light, a trick called "bioluminescence". To protect itself at night, the bobtail squid uses a glowing bacteria called *Vibrio fischeri*, which it houses in a small pouch on its mantle (body) called the light organ. The light it emits mimics the moonlight on the water, helping the squid to blend in with its surroundings, and allowing it to slip by predators unnoticed.

Luminous bacteria light up the squid's underside as it swims.

The light hides the squid's silhouette from predators below.

HOW TO KEEP FOOD FRESH

Before the 1860s, it was hard to keep milk for more than a few days. People had to buy it fresh every day, and even then it would sometimes make them sick. Milk spoiled very quickly, and nobody could figure out why, or how to prevent it from happening. Then, French biologist Louis Pasteur made a life-changing discovery that helped us to keep milk for longer, and make it safer.

1 Louis Pasteur began to study why drinks, and particularly milk, spoiled. Many people thought it was a random process, and also that risk of illness could not be avoided.

2 Pasteur soon realized that tiny microbes (microscopic organisms) found naturally in the milk were to blame for it spoiling, and that these also could make people ill.

3 He immediately started testing ways of killing the microbes. Soon, Pasteur discovered that boiling milk and then cooling it quickly made the milk last much longer than it had before, and stopped people getting ill when they drank it.

4 The process became known as "pasteurization". It was a huge success, and food producers began using it to stop other foods and drinks from spoiling, too. It is still used the world over.

Understanding the science
PASTEURIZATION

Pasteurization helps keep milk fresh for longer. It involves heating milk in a heat exchanger to a high temperature, and then quickly cooling it before sealing it in a bottle or a package that has been sterilized (cleared of microbes).

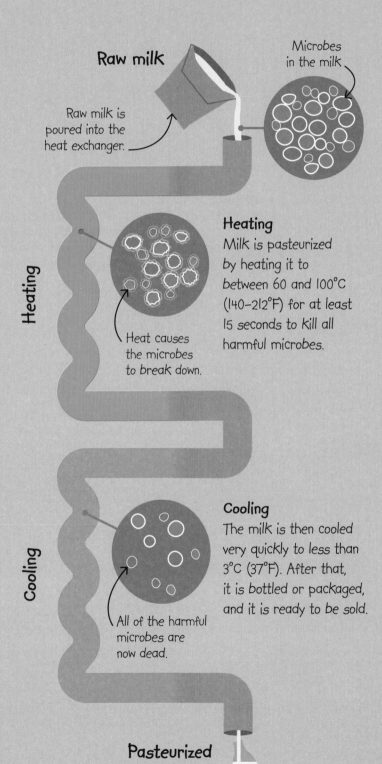

Raw milk

Microbes in the milk

Raw milk is poured into the heat exchanger.

Heating

Heating
Milk is pasteurized by heating it to between 60 and 100°C (140–212°F) for at least 15 seconds to kill all harmful microbes.

Heat causes the microbes to break down.

Cooling

Cooling
The milk is then cooled very quickly to less than 3°C (37°F). After that, it is bottled or packaged, and it is ready to be sold.

All of the harmful microbes are now dead.

Pasteurized milk is bottled

WHICH FOODS ARE PASTEURIZED?

Today, many of the foods we enjoy are pasteurized, though it is not always done for the same reasons. Most countries in the world now require many food products to be pasteurized in order for them to be sold to consumers.

Harmful microbes can't survive in honey, but pasteurization kills off yeasts that can spoil it.

Honey

Fruit juice

Cheese

Milk

While pasteurizing vinegar doesn't make it safer, it does add years to its lifetime.

Vinegar

Pasteurizing eggs kills off most of the bacteria and diseases that eggs can carry.

Eggs

Cream

TRY IT OUT
THE PH SCALE

The pH (potential of hydrogen) scale is a measure of how acidic or basic a liquid is. Acidic substances have a pH of 1–6, while pH 8–14 indicate basic substances. In this experiment, you will investigate what happens to the pH level of milk over time. You will need some litmus paper, which is used to measure pH level, and some milk.

Litmus paper comes in a book of short slips.

Pour a small amount of milk into a dish or jar.

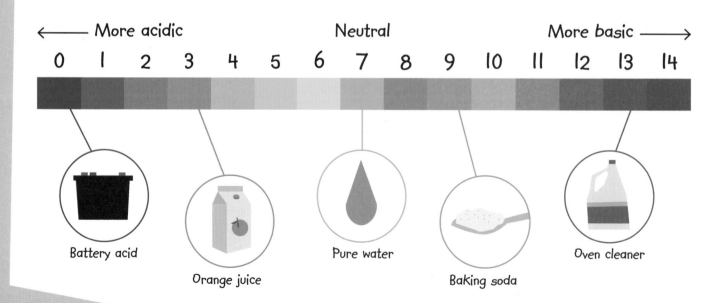

←— More acidic   Neutral   More basic —→

0 1 2 3 4 5 6 7 8 9 10 11 12 13 14

Battery acid

Orange juice

Pure water

Baking soda

Oven cleaner

WAR ON MICROBES

Foods have been preserved for centuries using a variety of methods such as drying, pickling, fermenting, and cooling. We now preserve food in even more ways, including canning, freezing, adding special chemicals, and by using advanced packaging materials. All either kill microbes, slow down microbes' ability to reproduce, or stop the food from being exposed to microbes before being eaten.

Use a litmus paper to test the milk, and record the result.

Leave the milk for at least a week (you might want to do this outside as it will smell!), and then test it with a different litmus paper.

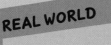

You should see that the pH level is lower than it was before. Even though the milk has been pasteurized, there are still some microbes left in it. Over time, they gradually multiply and produce lactic acid from the lactose in the milk, which makes the milk more acidic.

HOW TO SURVIVE

The animals and plants that lived on Earth millions of years ago were very different from those alive today. Over time, animals and plants can gradually change and develop into new species (types), a process called evolution. The first person to prove that evolution happens and to explain what causes it was the English naturalist Charles Darwin.

1 Darwin was fascinated by wildlife from an early age and dreamed of exotic travel. In 1831, when he was 22, he was invited to sail around the world as the naturalist on a scientific expedition. He jumped at the chance.

2 The five-year trip on HMS *Beagle* took Darwin to jungles, deserts, volcanoes, and tropical islands. He saw giant tortoises, marine iguanas, and other wonders. He kept a diary and made thousands of drawings and notes, recording all his observations with the utmost care.

3 In the Galápagos Islands – a cluster of volcanic islands in the Pacific Ocean – Darwin collected 13 new species of finch, each with a different kind of beak. Later, he wondered if they had a single ancestor that became marooned on the islands long ago.

4 After Darwin returned home, a theory about how evolution might work began to form in his mind. He spent years thinking it through and collecting evidence, but he was afraid to announce it as it went against religious beliefs. It wasn't until Darwin was 50 that he finally published his thoughts in a book. It was an instant bestseller and caused a scientific revolution.

Understanding the science
NATURAL SELECTION

Darwin saw that most organisms produce far more offspring than survive to reach adulthood and reproduce. This results in a kind of competition – a struggle to survive in which most offspring perish. Individuals with the best qualities have the greatest chance of winning and passing on their qualities to another generation. As Darwin realized, this means that nature continually weeds out the worst and selects the best. He called this "natural selection".

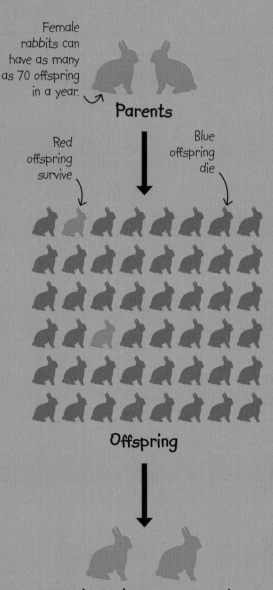

Female rabbits can have as many as 70 offspring in a year.

Parents

Red offspring survive

Blue offspring die

Offspring

Survivors become parents to next generation

DARWIN'S THEORY

Darwin's book said that evolution is mainly driven by natural selection, which causes species to change as they adapt to their environment. A famous example is the peppered moth, which can be pale or black. In the early 1800s, most peppered moths in English towns were pale, which provided good camouflage when they rested on tree bark. By the late 1800s, however, most peppered moths were black. Soot from factories had blackened trees, making the pale moths easier for birds to catch. Black moths now had the best camouflage and so won the struggle to survive, changing the species.

Pale peppered moths are well camouflaged on normal tree bark.

Black peppered moths are well camouflaged on sooty trees.

ADAPTATION OVER TIME

Darwin recognized that the finches he collected in the Galápagos were similar to a species in nearby South America. However, the island finches all had slightly different beaks. On each island, natural selection had favoured the birds with beaks best suited to the local diet. Those birds passed on their characteristics to the next generation, and the process kept repeating. Over time, each population had adapted to a different diet, evolving a unique kind of beak.

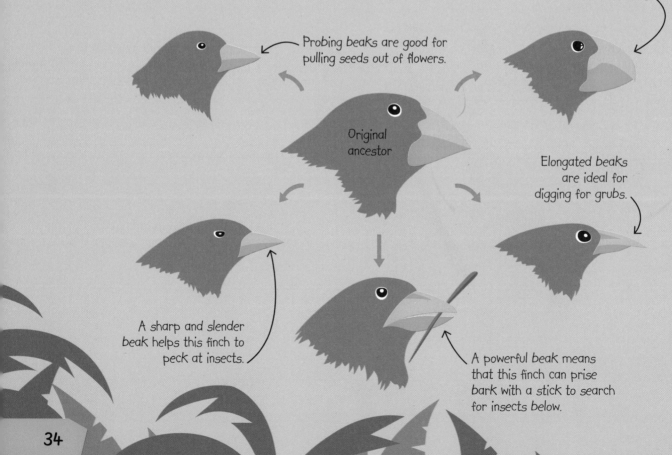

Probing beaks are good for pulling seeds out of flowers.

Hooked beak are suited to cutting into soft fruits and buds.

Original ancestor

Elongated beaks are ideal for digging for grubs.

A sharp and slender beak helps this finch to peck at insects.

A powerful beak means that this finch can prise bark with a stick to search for insects below.

HOW NEW SPECIES FORM

Darwin's voyage on HMS *Beagle* took him to remote islands, where he discovered species found nowhere else. He realized that new species can form if a population is split into isolated groups that can no longer interbreed. Over time, the process of evolution by natural selection changes each population in different ways until they become too different to breed with each other – they end up as different species.

Isolated populations eventually evolve into different species.

The two species remain distinct after mixing again.

1 A population of squirrels is spread across a continent. The squirrels can all interbreed, which means they form a single species.

2 Rising sea levels turn the mountains into isolated islands. Two separate populations now begin to evolve in different ways.

3 The sea level falls, allowing the squirrels to mix. However, they are now too different to breed: they have become separate species.

REAL WORLD

Courtship displays
The males of several bird species have elaborate courtship displays that involve dancing and showing colourful feathers to woo a female mate. The female always picks the best display. Over generations, this form of natural selection causes the males to become ever more eye-catching and their dances increasingly complex.

BRILLIANT BIOLOGISTS

Since ancient times, thinkers across the world have come up with ideas to explain how living things work and behave. Thanks to new technologies, such as the invention of the microscope, and the work of curious scientists on everything from how our *bodies* work to how *bees* communicate, our understanding has developed in leaps and bounds.

SUSHRUTA

Sushruta Samhita, compiled by the Indian physician Sushruta, is one of the earliest known medical books. It described more than 1,100 illnesses and 960 different medicinal uses for plants. Sushruta was also a pioneering surgeon and developed ways of performing operations, such as extracting teeth and removing cataracts (a condition where the lens of the eye gets cloudy).

4th century BCE

c. 1500 BCE

6th century BCE

MUCKY MEDICINE

In ancient Egypt, doctors recommended all sorts of unusual solutions for ailments and injuries. Ointments made from dung were popular treatments. Though this might sound revolting, we now know that some types of dung contain useful bacteria that can help kill harmful microorganisms.

FOUNDER OF BIOLOGY

The Greek philosopher Aristotle was the first person to attempt to classify living things. He grouped animals into those with blood and those without, and by observing live animals and making dissections on dead ones, he was one of the first people to realize that animals share common organs.

UNDER THE MICROSCOPE

Hans and Zacharias Janssen, a Dutch father-and-son team, invented the first compound microscope (a microscope with more than one lens) by placing two magnifying glasses in a tube. When they looked through it, objects at the other end appeared up to nine times larger.

1025 CE

1590s

1665

1735

DISCOVERING CELLS

The English scientist Robert Hooke first discovered cells when he shone a light through thinly cut pieces of cork under a compound microscope. Each tiny cell looked like a chamber with walls, which inspired Hooke to name them after *cellula*, the small rooms in a monastery.

MEDICAL MASTERPIECE

The Canon of Medicine by the Persian scholar Ibn Sina (also known as Avicenna) is one of the most important medical textbooks of all time. The book collected together medical knowledge from across the ancient and Islamic worlds, and was used by physicians for centuries after Ibn Sina's death.

A NEW SYSTEM

Frustrated by the chaotic way fellow scientists were naming plants, Swedish botanist and zoologist Carl Linnaeus devised a scientific system for classifying the natural world. Linnaeus divided all living things into two kingdoms (animals and plants), and then subdivided each one into more categories. His system is the basis of the one we use today.

BLOOD TYPES

The Austrian biologist Karl Landsteiner wondered why some blood transfusions (donations) were successful, while others could be deadly. Landsteiner discovered that human blood fell into at least three major types (A, B, and O); a year later, a fourth (AB) was found. For a transfusion to be successful, the patient's blood type must match that of their donor. This discovery has saved millions of lives.

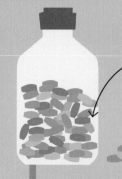

Some people need to supplement their diet with vitamin pills.

VITAL VITAMINS

While studying the disease beriberi, the Polish biochemist Casimir Funk realized that this and other life-threatening diseases such as scurvy were caused by diets lacking in vital substances that keep the body healthy. He called these "vital amines", which later became shortened to "vitamins".

1809

1839

1901

1912

CELL THEORY

By now, cells had been seen in many biological specimens through ever more powerful microscopes. The German scientists Thomas Schwann and Matthias Schleiden put forward the theory that all living things are made up of cells, and that cells are the basic building blocks of life.

DID YOU KNOW?

Wood Wide Web
Trees secretly talk to each other underground. Communicating through a network of fungi, they can share resources and spread information about dangers such as insect infestations. This global network has been nicknamed the "Wood Wide Web".

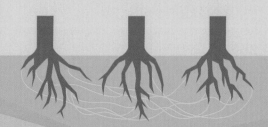

EVOLVING IDEAS

The French biologist Jean-Baptiste Lamarck came up with a theory of evolution before Charles Darwin. Lamarck thought that living things adopted new characteristics to adjust to their environment, and passed on the most useful ones to their offspring. We now know Lamarck's theory was oversimplified and that organisms don't inherit traits in quite this way.

Lamarck suggested that giraffes' necks have stretched through time to reach the highest leaves.

WAGGLE DANCE

The Austrian scientist Karl von Frisch discovered that when a honey *bee* finds food, it performs a dance to let the other bees in the hive know where to find it. The dance indicates the direction and distance of the food in relation to the Sun, and saves the other bees time and energy spent on searching for food. Scientists have used this discovery to better understand how bees and other animals communicate in large numbers.

DOLLY

Scientists successfully cloned (made a genetically identical copy of) a sheep from an adult cell. Cloning could help cure diseases, and might even one day be used to bring species back from extinction, but some people feel it goes against the way nature works.

The honey *bee's* "waggle" forms a figure of eight.

1916

1967

1972

1996

2009

ROBOTIC HAND

Three years after losing his forearm in a car crash, Pierpaolo Petruzziello became the first person able to control a robotic hand using just his mind. Scientists in Italy connected the hand to his nervous system using electrodes, and Petruzziello learned to feel sensations, wiggle a finger, and even grab hold of objects.

FIGHTING LEPROSY

In the early 20th century, leprosy – an infectious, painful, and sometimes disfiguring disease caused by bacteria – was believed to be almost untreatable. Aged just 24, the African American chemist Alice Ball pioneered an effective treatment for the disease, which was used until antibiotics made leprosy curable in the 1940s. Sadly, Ball died soon after her discovery and did not receive the recognition she deserved.

MALARIA TREATMENT

During the Vietnam War, Chinese chemist Tu Youyou was asked to find a treatment for malaria, which was killing many soldiers fighting for China's ally, North Vietnam. After testing thousands of treatments used in traditional Chinese medicine, Tu and her team identified one made from the leaves of sweet wormwood that really worked. Artemisinin, the drug she discovered, went on to save countless lives.

WHAT'S THE POINT OF
PHYSICS?

Without understanding physics, many of the things we take for granted today just wouldn't be possible. There would be no planes or smartphones – in fact, we wouldn't even be able to use electricity. Physics tackles major questions such as what makes objects fall down rather than up, and how do light and sound work? Physicists even think they might one day be able to unravel the ultimate mystery of the Universe – why does anything exist?

WHY DO WE NEED PHYSICS?

Want to know how the world works? Physics is a great start! Physics is at the heart of everything – it is the oldest science and the one on which all the others are built. Early physicists were people who simply questioned why the Universe worked the way it did – and tried to find ways of understanding it. That curiosity is still the biggest part of physics, and continues to lead to huge discoveries in many different fields.

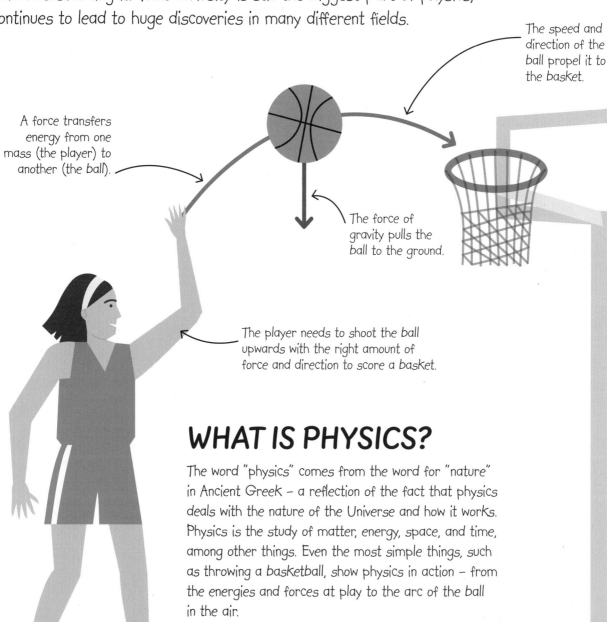

The speed and direction of the ball propel it to the basket.

A force transfers energy from one mass (the player) to another (the ball).

The force of gravity pulls the ball to the ground.

The player needs to shoot the ball upwards with the right amount of force and direction to score a basket.

WHAT IS PHYSICS?

The word "physics" comes from the word for "nature" in Ancient Greek – a reflection of the fact that physics deals with the nature of the Universe and how it works. Physics is the study of matter, energy, space, and time, among other things. Even the most simple things, such as throwing a basketball, show physics in action – from the energies and forces at play to the arc of the ball in the air.

WHAT'S THE POINT OF ATOMS?

Everything we see in the Universe, from a tiny ant to exploding stars to, is made up of atoms. They are building blocks of all matter. The word "atom" comes from the Ancient Greek for "not cuttable", because the ancient Greeks believed it could not be divided. We now know that the atom is made up of many smaller parts, which we call subatomic particles – protons and neutrons in the centre of the atom (which we call the nucleus), and electrons that spin around it.

Electrons travel around the nucleus in orbits.

Electrons carry a negative electric charge.

Protons (coloured blue) have a positive electric charge. Neutrons (in red) have no charge.

EVERYDAY PHYSICS

Physics has a hand in nearly everything around us – indeed, it's easier to spot what isn't in some way related to the subject. Many everyday things are powered by electricity, which clever physicists first learned to harness. Computers, TVs, and radios receive signals as invisible electromagnetic waves, another important area of physics.

Machines such as excavators use physics to turn small forces into big ones in order to do useful work.

The internet is made possible by satellites put into orbit around Earth, thanks to physics.

Aeroplanes use the laws of physics to get into the air, stay there without falling, and land safely.

Batteries store electrical energy, which can be used to power electric circuits to make them work.

Televisions work by using our knowledge of light, waves, and colour gained from physics.

WHAT POWERS THE WORLD?

People have known about electricity for thousands of years. The ancient Greeks experimented with static electricity, noticing how rubbing amber with fur created a charge. But it wasn't until centuries later that scientists realized electricity can flow through wires and transmit power. That discovery sparked an energy revolution that would reshape the whole world.

1 The people of ancient Egypt knew about electricity from the electric catfish they hunted in the Nile. They used electric shocks from the fish to treat arthritis.

Electric catfish use shocks to stun prey and to defend themselves.

2 By the middle of the 18th century, people had started to learn more about electricity. American inventor Benjamin Franklin even used it to kill and roast a turkey!

Understanding the science
BRIGHT SPARKS

Franklin's experiment proved that lightning and electricity were related. He proposed that electricity could flow like a liquid, moving from an area of negative charge to an area of positive charge. We now know the opposite is true: electricity flows from negative to positive.

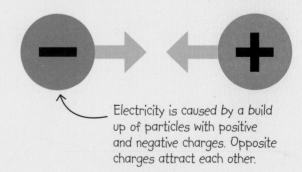

Electricity is caused by a build up of particles with positive and negative charges. Opposite charges attract each other.

3 Franklin had a theory that the lightning produced during thunderstorms was in fact a form of electricity. He devised an experiment to test his theory.

Franklin realized that bolts of lightning are giant electrical sparks.

A wire on the kite attracted electricity.

4 On a stormy day, he flew a kite with a key tied to the bottom of the string. When he went to touch the key, a spark flashed. His theory was correct.

Franklin collected the electric charge in a Leyden jar – an early sort of battery.

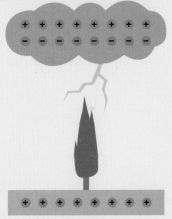

Thunderstorm

During a thunderstorm, a negative charge builds up on the base of the cloud and a positive charge builds up on the ground. They attract each other, creating a powerful charge. A lightning bolt is the attraction of the two forces.

Lightning conductor

Franklin's kite allowed some of the charge to flow to the ground. He was very lucky the kite wasn't struck by lightning – it would have killed him instantly.

STORING ELECTRICITY

Although Franklin coined the term "battery", it was the Italian inventor Alessandro Volta who invented the first working version in 1800. The voltaic pile used a chemical reaction to create electric charge and was the first battery able to supply an electric circuit with a continuous electric current.

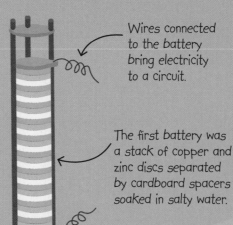

Wires connected to the battery bring electricity to a circuit.

The first battery was a stack of copper and zinc discs separated by cardboard spacers soaked in salty water.

POWERING EVERYONE

Vast amounts of electricity are produced every day in power stations to be transported far and wide by cables. Once electricity leaves the power station, the voltage (the force that makes an electric charge move) is increased ("stepped up") by transformers to reduce energy losses. The voltage is later reduced ("stepped down") to make it safe for use in homes.

Power stations use generators to create electricity.

Pylons keep dangerous power cables away from the ground.

Power station

Step-up transformer

Pylon

Step-down transformer

Home

REAL WORLD

Wonderful wind power
Most of the world's electricity is made by burning fossil fuels, but many countries are now turning to more environmentally friendly energy sources, such as wind and solar power.

ELECTRICITY AT HOME

Although early innovators like Franklin struggled to find a practical use for electricity, it ended up changing the entire world. From toasters and kettles, to fridges and phones, many of the devices we use every day are powered by electricity. It's difficult to imagine a world without it.

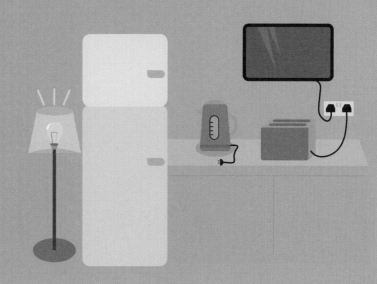

TRY IT OUT
STATIC ELECTRICITY

If you rub a balloon against a jumper or even your hair, the rubber will pick up particles and become negatively charged. Then, try picking up a piece of paper or moving an empty drink can with your statically charged balloon.

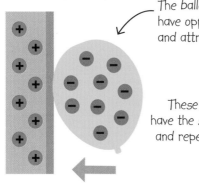

The balloon and wall have opposite charges and attract each other.

These two balloons have the same charge and repel each other.

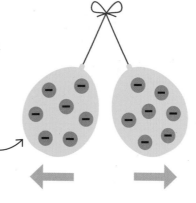

A charged balloon will stick to a wall as if by magic! This works because the balloon's negative charge repels negative particles in the wall, giving the wall's surface a positive charge.

Just as opposite charges attract, similar charges repel (push away) each other. If you hang two charged balloons side by side, the negative charges repel and the balloons separate.

1 Wilhelm Röntgen was carrying out experiments with a cathode ray tube – a glass tube that creates a beam of electrons (a cathode ray) when its electricity is switched on. Röntgen wanted to temporarily block all the rays from the tube, so he covered it in cardboard, which cathode rays can't pass through.

2 He switched on the tube and noticed a strange glow on a fluorescent screen in his lab. He turned off the tube and the screen went dark. Some kind of invisible rays must be passing through the cardboard. He had no idea what these invisible rays were, so he called them "X-rays".

HOW TO HAVE X-RAY VISION

X-rays were discovered by accident in 1895 by the German physicist Wilhelm Röntgen. Today they are used more than 100 million times a year in hospitals and dental surgeries all over the world. Like radio waves and light, X-rays are a form of energy called electromagnetic radiation. They have more energy than most other types of electromagnetic radiation, which allows them to pass straight through materials that visible light can't shine through – including human flesh. This makes X-rays ideal for looking inside the human body.

3 Röntgen found that his X-rays could pass through paper, books, and even thin bits of metal. He shone them through his wife's hand onto a photographic plate and made a shadow of her bones. "I have seen my death," she said after seeing the ghostly image. It was the world's first X-ray image of the human body.

HOW DO X-RAYS WORK?

X-ray images work in a very different way from photographs. A photographic image is made from light reflected by objects, but an X-ray image is made from electromagnetic radiation that has passed through objects. The white areas in an X-ray image are shadows caused by dense materials such as bone, which absorbs the radiation. Soft tissues, such as lungs or skin, only partially absorb X-rays and so appear grey. Dark areas are where the X-rays have passed right through – which is why X-rays are great at showing broken or fractured bones.

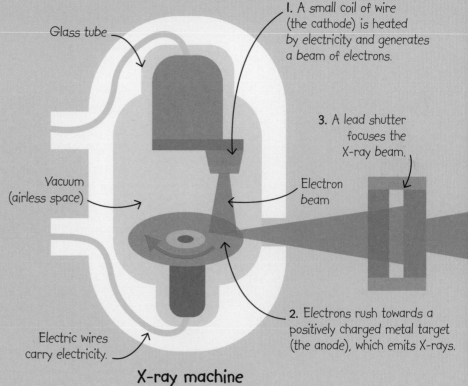

Glass tube

I. A small coil of wire (the cathode) is heated by electricity and generates a beam of electrons.

3. A lead shutter focuses the X-ray beam.

Vacuum (airless space)

Electron beam

Electric wires carry electricity.

2. Electrons rush towards a positively charged metal target (the anode), which emits X-rays.

X-ray machine

WHY ARE X-RAYS IMPORTANT?

X-rays are useful for finding problems with bones and teeth, but they can also help us catch terrorists or figure out the structure of molecules. It was thanks to X-rays that scientists first discovered the structure of DNA, the molecule that carries our genes.

CT scan of kidney

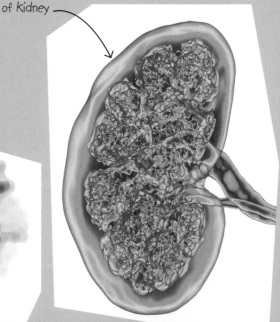

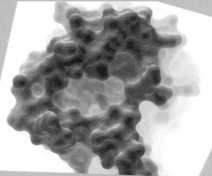

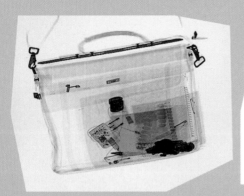

Airport security
X-ray scanners are used at airports to screen passengers' bags and bodies to see if they are carrying anything dangerous or illegal.

Molecular structure
X-rays, when fired at crystals and some other solids, scatter in distinctive patterns. Scientists can use these patterns to figure out the material's molecular structure.

CT scans
CT (computed tomography) machines are medical scanners that combine lots of X-rays taken from different angles to build up a detailed, 3D picture of the inside of the body.

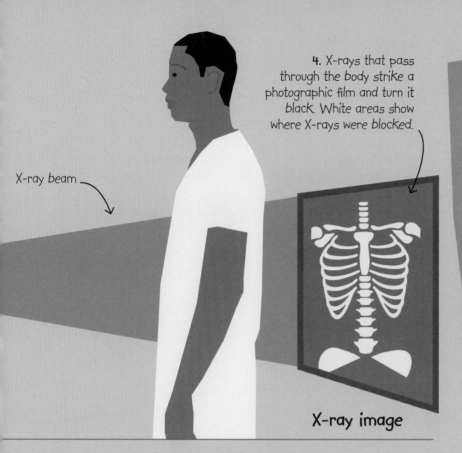

X-ray beam

4. X-rays that pass through the *body* strike a photographic film and turn it black. White areas show where X-rays were blocked.

X-ray image

X-rays in space

Stars and galaxies don't just emit visible light – they also produce X-rays. Astronomers use X-ray telescopes to study objects they can't *see* fully with visible light, such as *black holes* and the remains of exploded stars.

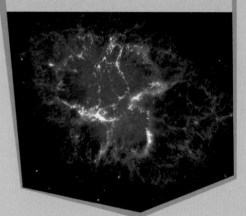

TRY IT OUT
SHADOW PLAY

X-rays are like visible light but can pass through objects more easily as they have more energy. To see how this works, all you need is a torch and a darkened room.

First, switch on the torch and stand in the beam. Your body absorbs or reflects all the light energy and so casts a shadow. This is how X-rays make images of dense materials like bone.

Next, put your hand over the beam. Your hand absorbs most of the energy but some gets through, which may make your skin glow. X-rays have more energy than visible light and so pass through soft tissues much more easily.

A powerful beam of light can pass through skin.

1 Ships once relied on people to spot icebergs, but at night these floating hazards are hard to see. Just before midnight on 14 April 1912, the *Titanic* struck an iceberg and sank, killing more than 1,500 people.

HOW TO SPOT A SUBMARINE

After an iceberg collision sank the *Titanic* in 1912, scientists began to explore ways of detecting obstacles hidden underwater. Two years later, World War I began and a new threat made the problem all the more urgent: submarine warfare. The solution was to borrow an ingenious idea from nature and "see" with sound instead of light. This system became known as sonar.

Submarines attacked merchant ships, which carried food and other home necessities.

2 In 1914, German submarines began to attack Allied (UK, US, French, and others) merchant ships crossing the Atlantic, making sea journeys even more hazardous.

Understanding the science
SEEING WITH SOUND

Bats and dolphins use a natural form of sonar, called echolocation or biosonar, to hunt prey in darkness or in murky water. They emit a stream of high-frequency clicks and listen for the echoes, which their brains then build into a kind of picture of where their prey is.

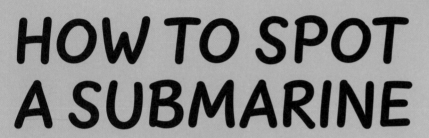

A dolphin makes clicking sounds up to 600 times a second.

The time it takes for an echo to return tells the dolphin how far away its prey is.

The sound waves bounce off prey as echoes. The direction of the echo reveals the prey's position.

Sound waves travel at 5,400 km/h (3,355 mph) in sea water.

3 By the start of World War II in 1939, Allied scientists had found a solution. They equipped warships with devices that sent beams of high-frequency (high-pitched) sound into the water. The sound waves bounced off enemy submarines and reflected back to a receiver on the ship.

4 A device in the ship's control room used the sound information to show the submarine's exact location. This allowed the crew to calculate where to drop "depth charges" – bombs that explode only when they sink to a particular depth. Now ships had a way of fighting back against the German submarines.

Bats can also "see" the speed and direction of movement of prey because a moving target changes the wavelength of the reflected sound. The sonar devices in warships used the same principle to calculate their target's position, speed, and direction.

A moth flying towards a bat squeezes reflected sound waves together, creating high-pitched echoes.

A moth flying away makes the reflected waves spread further apart, giving the sound a lower pitch.

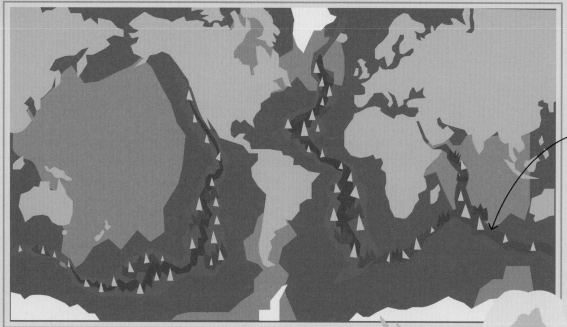

The mid-ocean ridge system is the world's longest mountain range.

UNDERSEA MOUNTAINS

By aiming sonar directly down from ships, scientists found they could measure the depth of the sea floor. This led to an amazing discovery, made by American scientist Marie Tharp in the 1950s: a hidden mountain chain runs through all of Earth's oceans. The discovery helped confirm a new theory that Earth's crust is broken into a jigsaw of moving plates, with the mountain range forming the boundary between major plates.

SONAR AND SEA LIFE

Today, fishing boats use sonar to decide where to cast their nets. Scientists also use sonar to monitor shoals of fish and make sure populations are not falling due to overfishing. But sonar may be harmful to some marine animals, such as dolphins and whales.

Fish-finding sonar is used to detect shoals of fish.

Some scientists think sonar from boats can frighten dolphins and whales and harm their ability to find prey.

54

RADAR

While sonar works well underwater, a similar system called radar works better to detect objects above ground. Radar uses radio waves, which travel at the speed of light and can reach further than sound waves. The air traffic control systems in airports use radar to monitor every plane that takes off and lands, coordinating flights to prevent collisions.

A radar device on the plane measures its height by bouncing radar signals off the ground.

The position of each plane appears as a dot on the radar display in the airport's control tower.

A second antenna collects information about the plane's height and identity.

ESE002

A radar antenna on the ground sends out radio waves, and picks up the reflections coming back at it.

REAL WORLD

Ultrasound scanning
An ultrasound scanner is a machine that uses echoes to look inside the human body. Doctors use ultrasound scans to check that babies are developing normally inside the mother's body and to find out whether a baby is a boy or a girl. The scanner uses very high-frequency sound waves that our ears cannot hear.

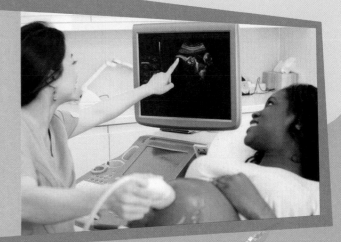

FANTASTIC PHYSICISTS

From the earliest days, people have used the ideas of physics in everyday life, from building simple machines to understanding gravity. Brilliant minds have led us to a greater understanding of how things work, from energy to motion, and from light to sound. Today, the boundaries of physics grow ever wider, as scientists tackle mind-boggling questions about space and time.

ANCIENT ATOMS

Ancient thinkers came up with theories that influence our understanding of atoms today. The Indian philosopher Kanada suggested that all things were composed of indestructible particles combined in different ways. Democritus, a Greek philosopher, had similar ideas about an infinite number of indivisible particles, which he called *atomos* after the Greek for "not cuttable".

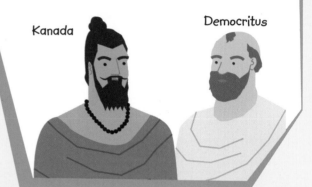

Kanada

Democritus

c. 2000 BCE

4th century BCE

c. 200 BCE

EARLY LEVERS

Levers are simple machines that use the principles of physics to make lifting easier. The ancient Mesopotamians and Egyptians used a device called a *shaduf* to help lift water from a river to irrigate their fields. The machine is still used in some rural societies today.

The farmer pulls down on a rope to lower the bucket into the water.

When the farmer releases the rope, a counterweight lifts the filled bucket back up.

THE FIRST COMPASS

The ancient Chinese developed a type of compass using a magnetic stone called a lodestone, which was carved into the shape of a spoon and placed on a bronze plate. As the plate was moved, the lodestone would spin round, with its handle always pointing to the south.

The plate was marked with the eight compass points.

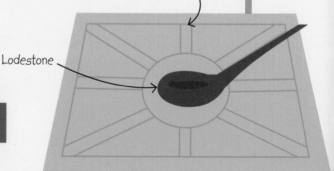

Lodestone

UNDERSTANDING VISION

The Arab scholar Hasan Ibn al-Haytham transformed our understanding of light and vision. Since ancient times, scholars had believed that we see because the eye emits light. Ibn al-Haytham explained how in fact light rays are reflected from an object into the eye, which then creates an image of the object. He went on to explain shadows, eclipses, and rainbows.

DID YOU KNOW?

The Scientific Revolution
In Europe, ideas from ancient Greece tended to dominate how people thought of the world. From the 1540s onwards, scholars began to question these older ideas, and come up with new ways of looking at the world based on observations and experiments. We now call this period "The Scientific Revolution".

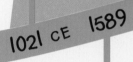

1021 CE   1589

1670s

FALLING OBJECTS

Galileo Galilei, an Italian astronomer and mathematician, was one of the first scientists to test his theories by experiment. Aristotle had argued that if dropped from a height, heavy objects would fall more quickly than lighter ones. Galileo didn't agree and designed an experiment in which he would drop two cannonballs of different masses from the famous Leaning Tower of Pisa. Galileo's theory was correct, and showed that gravity exerts the same pull on all objects, regardless of their mass.

In Galileo's experiment, both balls reached the ground at the same time.

NEWTON'S APPLE

When seeing an apple fall from a tree in his grandmother's orchard, Isaac Newton wondered why it would always fall to the ground, rather than up into the sky or to the side. His interest led to a deeper understanding of gravity, and how it causes the orbits of planets and moons.

LIGHT WAVES

Since ancient times, scientists had argued over two theories of light. The English scientist Isaac Newton thought that light is made up of a stream of tiny particles. A Dutch scientist, Christiaan Huygens, disagreed. He argued instead that light travels as waves, like ripples across the surface of water. In fact, both scientists were correct, as we now know that light behaves both like waves and like particles.

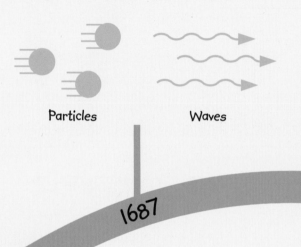

Particles   Waves

THEORY OF RELATIVITY

Albert Einstein's work transformed our understanding of the Universe. His famous equation, $E=mc^2$, showed that matter (mc^2) can be turned into energy (E) and back. Later, he showed how light, time, and space are affected by gravity. His theories also led scientists to understand and explore mysterious things such as black holes and the Big Bang.

1687   1831   1905–1917

DID YOU KNOW?

The speed of light

After studying the eclipses of Jupiter's moon Io, in 1676 the Danish astronomer Ole Rømer reversed centuries of thinking when he showed that the speed of light was not infinite, and could be measured. It took scientists another 300 years to agree on an exact measurement, which is almost 300,000 kilometres per second (186,000 miles per second).

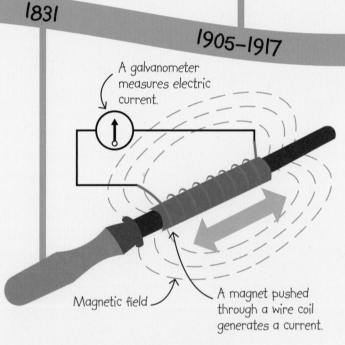

A galvanometer measures electric current.

Magnetic field

A magnet pushed through a wire coil generates a current.

ELECTROMAGNETISM

The English scientist Michael Faraday made an important link between electricity and magnets. He discovered that by pushing a magnet through a tube wrapped in a coil of wire, an electric current could be created. Faraday had invented the first generator. Today, the electricity that powers our homes comes from generators based on Faraday's invention.

NUCLEAR FISSION

When working with the element uranium, the German physicists Lise Meitner and Otto Frisch discovered it was possible to split an atomic nucleus into smaller nuclei, causing a reaction that releases a huge amount of energy. This process, called nuclear fission, was developed to generate nuclear power – and also led to the creation of the atomic bomb.

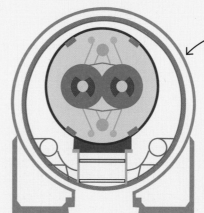

The LHC is a circular magnet tunnel, 27 km (15 miles) long.

THEORY OF EVERYTHING

Scientists have tried to re-create the conditions of the Big Bang – a massive explosion thought to have started the Universe – by building the world's largest machine on the Franco-Swiss border. Inside the machine, called the Large Hadron Collider (LHC), tiny particles called hadrons are smashed together at almost the speed of light. Scientists hope this might one day lead to an explanation of how every aspect of physics in the Universe works – a theory of everything.

1911 **1938** **2008** **2019**

ATOMIC NUCLEUS

From ancient times, scientists thought that atoms were the smallest units of matter and couldn't be broken down further. Then the New Zealander Ernest Rutherford and his colleagues discovered that inside the atom were even tinier charged particles: negatively charged electrons and, at its core, a tiny nucleus bound by an incredibly strong force. Later research showed that the nucleus could be subdivided further.

BLACK HOLES

Einstein's theories had led scientists to establish the existence of black holes – regions of space where gravity is so strong that nothing, not even light, can escape. Katie Bouman, an American computer scientist, developed a program that led to the first ever picture taken of a black hole.

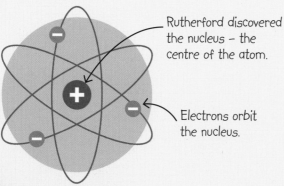

Rutherford discovered the nucleus – the centre of the atom.

Electrons orbit the nucleus.

Rutherford's model of the atom

WHAT'S THE POINT OF
CHEMISTRY?

Chemistry looks at what things are made of – starting with atoms, the basic building blocks of life – and how they can be combined in different ways to make new things. Understanding these processes has helped modern chemists improve our lives in many ways, from creating medicines to keep us healthy to making our farming methods more productive so that we all have enough to eat.

WHY DO WE NEED CHEMISTRY?

Atoms, reactions, and changes in state are at the heart of chemistry. Chemistry looks at what different things are made of, and how they behave in different circumstances – what happens when they are combined or separated, or when they are heated or cooled, for example? Chemistry is incredibly important to everyday life. It has helped us to create fuels for cars and planes, and to make the food we eat taste good and last longer.

WHAT IS CHEMISTRY?

Chemistry is the study of the characteristics and structure of matter. Everything contains atoms, but the ways in which they are arranged dictate how a substance behaves. In this way, chemistry is just like cooking – heating or cooling different ingredients results in a different dish, and some ingredients, like water, can be used in different ways as a solid, a liquid, or a gas.

In gases, such as steam, particles are spaced far apart and move about quickly – this is why they spread out.

Boiling water makes its particles move faster, so it changes state into steam.

Freezing water turns it into solid ice. In a solid, the substance's atoms are bonded tightly together, and hold their shape.

Changing temperature changes a substance's state.

The atoms in liquid water can move around freely, which is why they flow easily.

EVERYDAY CHEMISTRY

Chemistry has led to the creation of lots of important new substances that are useful in our daily lives, but also has led us to understand the way living things work, too. In fact, it's the chemical changes, or reactions, that take place in our bodies – from digesting food to powering our muscles – that help to keep us alive!

Understanding what happens when chemical substances are mixed together has helped scientists develop effective new medicines.

Chemists study the features of different materials, such as their hardness. Diamond is the hardest natural substance found on Earth.

The first plastic was invented in a laboratory more than a century ago. Plastics are made of natural materials such as crude oil and gas.

Party balloons filled with helium gas float because helium is much lighter than nitrogen or oxygen, the two main gases in the air.

Fire is a chemical reaction, and so is putting it out. When water hits fire, it boils and turns to steam, which floats off and takes the heat with it.

WHAT'S THE POINT OF ELEMENTS?

Elements are pure substances, made up of a single type of atom. There are 118 elements, and each one has unique features. When the atoms in elements join together, whether from one element or different ones, they form molecules.

A water molecule (H_2O) is made of two hydrogen atoms and one oxygen atom.

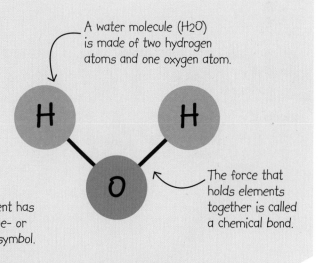

H H

O

The force that holds elements together is called a chemical bond.

Every element has its own atomic number – this is the number of protons in the nucleus of an atom of the element.

Each element has a unique one- or two-letter symbol.

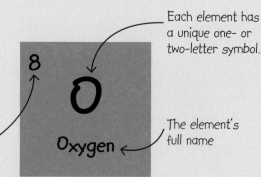

8

O

Oxygen

The element's full name

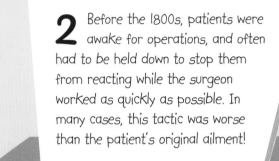

1 In ancient Egypt, physicians sometimes applied pressure to an artery in a patient's arm or leg before an operation. This made the limb "fall asleep" so the patient couldn't feel anything. In 1700s Europe, some doctors tried hypnotism to relax patients, with limited success.

2 Before the 1800s, patients were awake for operations, and often had to be held down to stop them from reacting while the surgeon worked as quickly as possible. In many cases, this tactic was worse than the patient's original ailment!

HOW TO STOP THE PAIN

Before the 19th century, surgery was usually a gruesome and painful procedure. As doctors and surgeons hacked off limbs or sewed up wounds, they tried a variety of methods to distract patients from the agony they were inflicting on them. Then, in the early 1800s, scientists began to experiment with the effects of inhaling different gases, which caused a loss of sensation in the patient. It was a medical breakthrough that provided relief for patients, and enabled doctors and surgeons to concentrate solely on getting their work done.

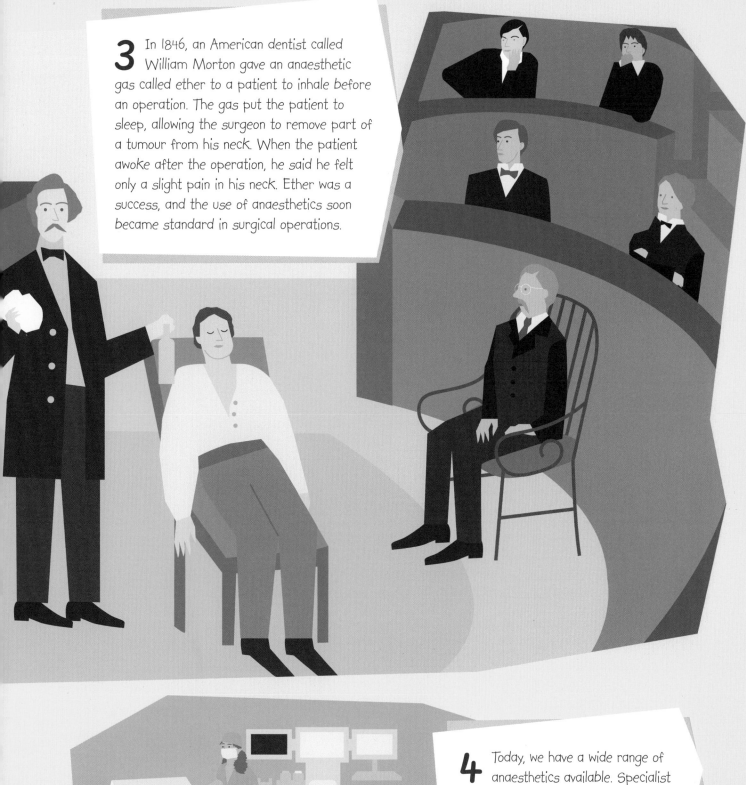

3 In 1846, an American dentist called William Morton gave an anaesthetic gas called ether to a patient to inhale before an operation. The gas put the patient to sleep, allowing the surgeon to remove part of a tumour from his neck. When the patient awoke after the operation, he said he felt only a slight pain in his neck. Ether was a success, and the use of anaesthetics soon became standard in surgical operations.

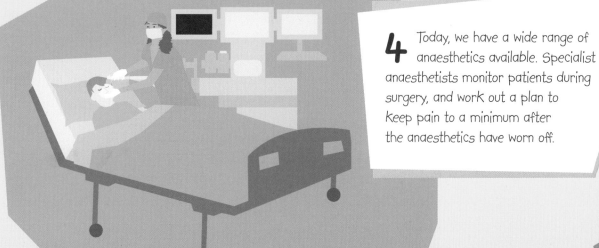

4 Today, we have a wide range of anaesthetics available. Specialist anaesthetists monitor patients during surgery, and work out a plan to keep pain to a minimum after the anaesthetics have worn off.

WHAT IS PAIN?

Pain is our body's warning system that something is wrong. When we feel pain, we feel a sensation in special nerve cells called pain receptors. These release a chemical that sends messages through our nervous system to our brain to tell us that we need to do something to stop the pain.

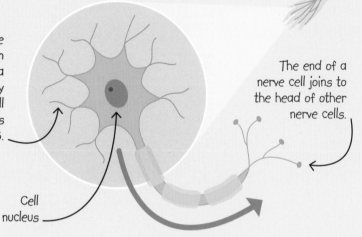

The central nervous system (CNS) is made up of the brain and the spinal cord.

When a nerve cell picks up a pain sensation, it passes a signal along its body to the next nerve cell until the signal gets to the CNS.

The end of a nerve cell joins to the head of other nerve cells.

The peripheral nervous system branches out from the CNS to the rest of the body.

Cell nucleus

HOW ANAESTHETICS WORK

These days, anaesthetics can be used to numb an area of your body (called a local anaesthetic) or completely put you to sleep (general anaesthetic) for a set amount of time. After the anaesthetic wears off, nerve signals are able to reach the brain, and a patient regains consciousness and feeling.

Normally, areas of the brain "talk" to each other by sending signals back and forth.

A general anaesthetic slows messages getting to and being sent by the brain.

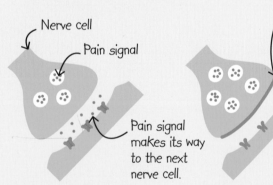

Nerve cell

Pain signal

Local anaesthetic blocks the pain signal's path so it does not travel further.

Pain signal makes its way to the next nerve cell.

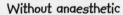

Without anaesthetic   **With anaesthetic**

Without anaesthetic   **With anaesthetic**

Local anaesthetics

There is a small gap between one nerve cell and the next that the pain signal must cross to be felt. A local anaesthetic blocks this from happening.

General anaesthetics

Patients lose all consciousness under a general anaesthetic. Scientists don't fully understand why it works, but it might have something to do with calming the brain's signals.

WHAT HAPPENS DURING SURGERY?

An anaesthetist is a doctor who specializes in giving patients anaesthetics. They tailor the dose of an anaesthetic to the patient so they lose consciousness and do not wake up during the procedure. During a general anaesthetic, the anaesthetist stays with the patient to make sure that the patient's heart rate, oxygen levels, and other vital signs are healthy.

Your brain calms and stops responding to pain signals. When you wake, you feel as if you fell asleep only moments ago.

Muscle relaxants are included with a general anaesthetic. These cause your muscles to completely relax, so they do not react to the sensation of the operation.

Your heart rate is monitored to ensure it remains constant and blood keeps flowing at a healthy rate.

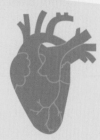

GOING TO THE DENTIST

Dentists can give you a general or local anaesthetic, depending on your treatment, but they can also give you "laughing gas". This is inhaled with some oxygen and makes most people feel more relaxed and sometimes a little silly!

The dentist may inject a local anesthetic into your gum before a treatment.

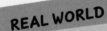

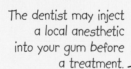

"Laughing gas" is most often inhaled through the nose to allow the dentist to work on your teeth.

REAL WORLD

Living longer
Anaesthetics are one of the big improvements that revolutionized health care. Now, people who have good access to health care can expect to live to be 80 or more, and have a great quality of life.

CAN YOU MAKE GOLD?

For more than 1,000 years, the scholars of the ancient world searched for the "philosopher's stone" – a mythical substance with the power to transform worthless metals into valuable gold. They failed, but their efforts didn't go to waste. In his hunt for gold, the Persian scientist Jabir ibn Hayyan devised many ingenious inventions and processes that are still used in labs today.

Jabir thought that by combining sulphur and mercury, he could make any metal – even gold.

1 For centuries, alchemists (early scientists who believed in magic) tried to transform "base metals" such as lead into "noble metals" like gold and silver. They had no idea that this was impossible.

2 Unlike earlier scholars, Jabir thought the answer lay in doing experiments. He carried out endless tests, discovering new chemicals and techniques, and recorded all his results carefully.

3 He is credited with writing hundreds of books detailing his discoveries. These paved the way for chemistry to develop into a modern science based on experiments, leaving behind the age of magic and superstition.

The retort is used to separate liquids by heating them.

Jabir invented 20 types of chemistry lab equipment and used them to develop processes such as crystallization, sublimation, evaporation, and distillation.

THE SCIENTIFIC METHOD

Jabir helped to lead science away from magic by using experiments to make discoveries about how things work. Experiments are at the heart of what we now call the scientific method: a step-by-step process that scientists use to form ideas and then test them to see if they're true. Without the scientific method, we wouldn't have the knowledge or science we have today.

The scientific method starts with a question. For example, why is pond water green?

Ask a question

Do background research

A hypothesis is a possible explanation. Maybe pond water is green because there are microscopic plants living in it.

Make a hypothesis

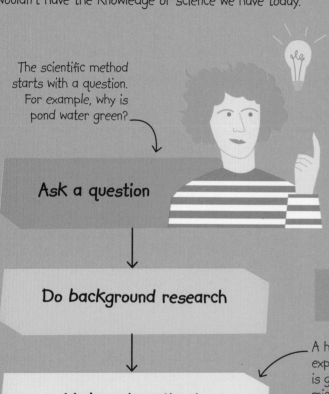

An experiment gathers data (information) to test the hypothesis.

Sometimes experiments fail because of faulty equipment or methods.

Test with an experiment

Is the procedure working?

Yes

No

Troubleshoot procedure. Carefully check all steps and setup

TRY IT OUT
BECOME A SCIENTIST

Think of a question you'd like to know the answer to, then follow the scientific method to see what you can figure out. Can you study which objects float in a bowl of water? And can you then form a hypothesis to predict what makes certain objects float?

Data from experiment becomes background information for new research. Ask new question, form new hypothesis, experiment again!

Graphs and charts help scientists spot patterns in data.

Analyse data and draw conclusions

Results support hypothesis.

Results align partially or not at all with hypothesis

Share results

Good scientists write up their experiments for other scientists to read about and repeat.

HOW TO PREDICT THE FUTURE

Everything that exists on Earth, in our bodies, and in the Universe is made up of the tiny building blocks of matter we call atoms. We know of 118 different kinds of atom, and each type is known as a chemical element. When all the elements are listed by the size of their atoms, they form a repeating pattern that we organize into a chart called the periodic table. The creation of this table in 1869 was one of the greatest breakthroughs in the history of chemistry.

1 By the 1860s, chemists had discovered and named about 60 elements. They had even calculated the atomic weight of each element relative to hydrogen, the lightest element. But it took the genius of Dmitri Mendeleev, a Russian chemist, to spot the pattern hidden in the numbers.

2 Mendeleev said that his discovery came to him in a dream. He saw the elements arranged by order of atomic weight, but in a table, so that elements with similar chemical properties lined up in columns.

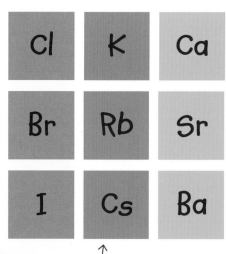

Mendeleev's dream revealed just a handful of elements arranged in order of atomic weight.

Cl	K	Ca
Br	Rb	Sr
I	Cs	Ba

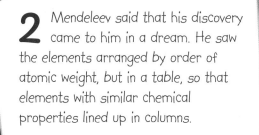

Mendeleev's first attempt at the table used dashes (—) for elements that had not been discovered yet.

H							
Li	Be	B	C	N	O	F	
Na	Mg	Al	Si	P	S	Cl	
K	Ca	—	Ti	V	Cr	Mn	Fe Co Ni Cu
(Cu)	Zn	—	—	As	Se	Br	
Rb	Sr	?Yt	Zr	Nb	Mo	—	Ru Rh Pd Ag
	Cd	In	Sn	Sb	Te	J	— —
Ba	?Di	?Ce	—	—	—	—
—	—	—	—	—	—	Os Ir Pt Au
Au							— —
—							

3 But the table only worked if he left gaps in it. He announced that the gaps were undiscovered elements, and he predicted their properties. Within a few years the first three of these were found, proving Mendeleev right.

THE INGREDIENTS OF EVERYTHING

Since Mendeleev's time, many new elements have been discovered, giving today's table 118 elements. The periodic table hasn't just helped scientists find new elements. It also helped them figure out the structure of atoms, which we now know are made of even tinier particles called protons, neutrons, and electrons. The modern table is arranged by the number of protons in atoms rather than atomic weight. Elements in the same column share similar chemical properties because they have the same number of outer electrons available to form bonds with other atoms.

1 **H** Hydrogen									
3 **Li** Lithium	4 **Be** Beryllium								
11 **Na** Sodium	12 **Mg** Magnesium								
19 **K** Potassium	20 **Ca** Calcium	21 **Sc** Scandium	22 **Ti** Titanium	23 **V** Vanadium	24 **Cr** Chromium	25 **Mn** Manganese	26 **Fe** Iron	27 **Co** Cobalt	28 **Ni** Nickel
37 **Rb** Rubidium	38 **Sr** Strontium	39 **Y** Yttrium	40 **Zr** Zirconium	41 **Nb** Niobium	42 **Mo** Molybdenum	43 **Tc** Technetium	44 **Ru** Ruthenium	45 **Rh** Rhodium	46 **Pd** Palladium
55 **Cs** Caesium	56 **Ba** Barium	57-71 **La-Lu**	72 **Hf** Hafnium	73 **Ta** Tantalum	74 **W** Tungsten	75 **Re** Rhenium	76 **Os** Osmium	77 **Ir** Iridium	78 **Pt** Platinum
87 **Fr** Francium	88 **Ra** Radium	89-103 **Ac-Lr**	104 **Rf** Rutherfordium	105 **Db** Dubnium	106 **Sg** Seaborgium	107 **Bh** Bohrium	108 **Hs** Hassium	109 **Mt** Meitnerium	110 **Ds** Darmstadtium

57 **La** Lanthanum	58 **Ce** Cerium	59 **Pr** Praseodymium	60 **Nd** Neodymium	61 **Pm** Promethium	62 **Sm** Samarium	63 **Eu** Europium
89 **Ac** Actinium	90 **Th** Thorium	91 **Pa** Protactinium	92 **U** Uranium	93 **Np** Neptunium	94 **Pu** Plutonium	95 **Am** Americium

All of the elements in the first column have one electron in their outermost shell.

PRECIOUS METALS

Gold, silver, and copper are among the few elements found in nature in their pure form. As a result, these metals have been used for centuries: gold and silver for jewellery because of their colour and shine, and copper for tools and coins because it's easy to shape and then harden. Silver also kills germs, which made it useful for handling or storing food. People even dropped silver coins into barrels of water and milk to help keep them fresh.

Today's periodic table shows elements in order of atomic number (the number of protons in an atom's nucleus).

Nonmetals are shown in blue. All other elements are either metals or have metallic properties.

							2 **He** Helium
5 **B** Boron	6 **C** Carbon	7 **N** Nitrogen	8 **O** Oxygen	9 **F** Fluorine	10 **Ne** Neon		
13 **Al** Aluminium	14 **Si** Silicon	15 **P** Phosphorus	16 **S** Sulphur	17 **Cl** Chlorine	18 **Ar** Argon		

29 **Cu** Copper	30 **Zn** Zinc	31 **Ga** Gallium	32 **Ge** Germanium	33 **As** Arsenic	34 **Se** Selenium	35 **Br** Bromine	36 **Kr** Krypton
47 **Ag** Silver	48 **Cd** Cadmium	49 **In** Indium	50 **Sn** Tin	51 **Sb** Animony	52 **Te** Tellurium	53 **I** Iodine	54 **Xe** Xenon
79 **Au** Gold	80 **Hg** Mercury	81 **Tl** Thallium	82 **Pb** Lead	83 **Bi** Bismuth	84 **Po** Polonium	85 **At** Astatine	86 **Rn** Radon
111 **Rg** Roentgenium	112 **Cn** Copernicium	113 **Nh** Nihonium	114 **Fl** Flerovium	115 **Mc** Moscovium	116 **Lv** Livermorium	117 **Ts** Tennessine	118 **Og** Oganesson

64 **Gd** Gadolinium	65 **Tb** Terbium	66 **Dy** Dysprosium	67 **Ho** Holmium	68 **Er** Erbium	69 **Tm** Thulium	70 **Yb** Ytterbium	71 **Lu** Lutetium
96 **Cm** Curium	97 **Bk** Berkelium	98 **Cf** Californium	99 **Es** Einsteinium	100 **Fm** Fermium	101 **Md** Mendelevium	102 **No** Nobelium	103 **Lr** Lawrencium

Periods

Horizontal rows are called periods. All elements in a period have the same number of electron shells in their atoms.

Periods run from left to right.

Groups

Vertical columns are called groups. The elements in a group have the same number of electrons in their outermost shell, giving them similar chemical properties.

Groups run from top to bottom.

KEY

 Nonmetals

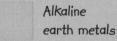 Alkali metals

Alkaline earth metals

Transition metals

Metalloids

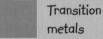 Post-transition metals

 Rare earth and actinide metals

REAL WORLD

Helium

Helium is the second lightest element, which makes it ideal for filling balloons as this colourless, odourless gas is lighter than air. It's also very safe as it's the second-least reactive element. Hydrogen is lighter but is highly flammable.

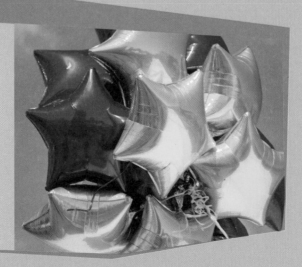

HOW TO LIGHT UP THE SKY

The deafening bang and dazzling flash of a firework come from energy released by a rapid chemical reaction. The first fireworks were made in ancient China after a chance discovery led to the invention of gunpowder. The discovery didn't just give the world sound and light shows – it also gave us guns, cannons, rockets, and bombs, forever changing the way wars were fought.

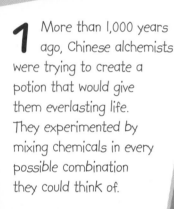

1 More than 1,000 years ago, Chinese alchemists were trying to create a potion that would give them everlasting life. They experimented by mixing chemicals in every possible combination they could think of.

2 One unlucky alchemist mixed up charcoal, sulphur, and potassium nitrate and then heated it. The concoction exploded and burned down his house. He had discovered gunpowder!

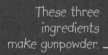
These three ingredients make gunpowder.

Potassium nitrate

Charcoal

Sulphur

Understanding the science
CHEMICAL REACTIONS

When chemicals react, their molecules are broken apart and the atoms rearrange to make new molecules. Some chemical reactions happen slowly, as when iron rusts, but others take place in an instant. Fireworks are powered by reactions that are not only fast but also release huge amounts of energy. The sudden release of energy causes a rapid expansion of gas – an explosion.

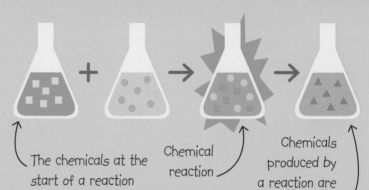

The chemicals at the start of a reaction are called reactants.

Chemical reaction

Chemicals produced by a reaction are called products.

3 Exactly who made the first firework is a mystery. One story says that a monk called Li Tan filled bamboo with gunpowder and threw it into a fire, resulting in a shower of sparks and a BANG!

The heat of a fire is needed to ignite gunpowder.

4 It wasn't long before fireworks became popular at festivities. People mounted them on arrows to make rockets that shot into the sky. Over time, the explosions became bigger, brighter, louder, and more colourful.

Chemical energy

All molecules contain hidden energy trapped in the bonds between atoms. During a chemical reaction, some of this energy can escape as heat, light, or sound. Chemical reactions that release energy, such as a candle burning, are called exothermic. Chemical reactions that take in energy, such as ice melting, are endothermic.

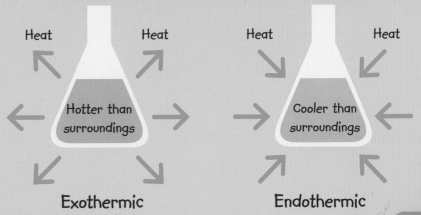

Heat   Heat

Hotter than surroundings

Exothermic

Heat   Heat

Cooler than surroundings

Endothermic

HOW DO FIREWORKS WORK?

Modern rocket fireworks have two main compartments of gunpowder: one to launch the firework and another to create the colourful display. The most sophisticated fireworks are packed with mini fireworks that shoot off in different directions and then explode in a carefully timed sequence.

Rocket fireworks reach the speed of jet fighter planes.

The bottom section of fuse burns for 3–9 seconds.

1 The first part of a rocket firework to burn is the fuse. This burns slowly, creating a delay that allows the firework to be safely lit and controlling when other parts of the firework ignite.

2 Next, gunpowder packed into the rocket's base ignites. It burns explosively, pushing hot gases out from the bottom and so propelling the rocket upwards at great speed.

WHAT IS COMBUSTION?

Fireworks depend on a chemical reaction called combustion (burning). Combustion requires three things: a fuel, oxygen (which reacts with the fuel), and a source of heat to start the reaction. In most combustion reactions the oxygen comes from air, but explosives such as gunpowder contain chemicals that release oxygen chemically, making the reaction faster.

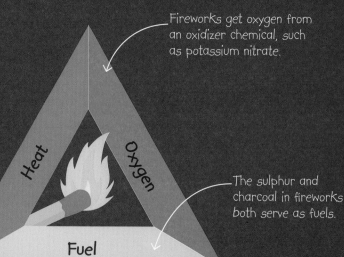

Fireworks get oxygen from an oxidizer chemical, such as potassium nitrate.

The sulphur and charcoal in fireworks both serve as fuels.

A source of heat is needed to start a combustion reaction.

Heat

Oxygen

Fuel

The way stars are packed together affects the shapes they make in the sky.

REAL WORLD

Dynamite

Explosives are used to blast passages through mountains, demolish buildings, excavate mines, and set off controlled avalanches. One of the most common explosives is dynamite, which was invented by the Swedish chemist Alfred Nobel as a safer alternative to gunpowder. Nobel used the fortune he made from explosives to establish the Nobel Prizes.

3 Finally, the top of the rocket ignites. It contains dozens of small packets of explosive called stars. These burst outwards as they burn, creating streaks of coloured light and booming explosions or crackling sounds.

COLOURS!

Fireworks get their brilliant colours from various metal compounds added to the gunpowder. When metal atoms heat up, they become "excited", which means that electrons jump to higher orbits. The electrons then return to their lower orbits and release energy as light. The light's colour depends on the type of metal used in the firework – for example, magnesium produces white light.

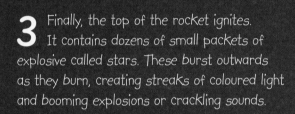
Magnesium

Copper

Strontium

Barium

Sodium

Calcium

WHAT'S UP WITH PLASTIC?

Plastic is an incredibly useful material found everywhere in the modern world. Some of its uses are obvious, such as food packaging, but there are many everyday items you may not even realize are made out of plastic, such as clothing or even paint. The chemical make-up of plastic is similar to that of some natural materials, like silk and rubber, but plastics are a human invention, first cooked up by a Belgian-born scientist.

1 In the early 20th century, people became ever more reliant on electricity. Electrical wires need to be insulated to work safely and effectively. Manufacturers used an expensive substance called shellac for insulation.

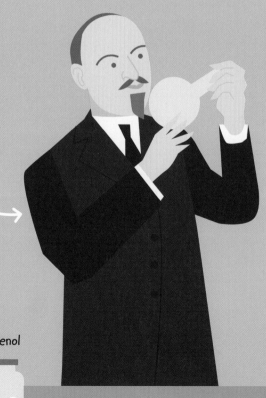

Shellac is a natural substance produced by the female lac bug.

Shellac forms plastic-like pieces, which can be dissolved in ethanol (alcohol) to make liquid shellac.

Electrical wires were dipped in liquid shellac to insulate them.

2 In the US, the chemist Leo Hendrik Baekeland began experimenting with chemicals to create a synthetic (artificial) version of shellac that could be mass-produced.

He used a type of pressure cooker that he invented, which he called a Bakelizer.

Formaldehyde

Phenol

80

3 By mixing two chemicals, formaldehyde and phenol, together at a carefully controlled temperature and pressure in the Bakelizer, he created the world's first synthetic polymer, or plastic.

4 Baekeland named this strong, light material Bakelite. It was great for insulating electrical wires, but it was so versatile that it could be moulded to make dozens of other items, too.

Telephones

Hair dryers

Jewellery

Chess pieces

Radios

Electric fans

Cameras

Understanding the science
POLYMERS

Shellac and Bakelite are both made up of polymers – long chains of smaller molecules joined together in a repeating pattern. These smaller molecules are known as monomers, and they work like building blocks. Here is one example of an ethene monomer.

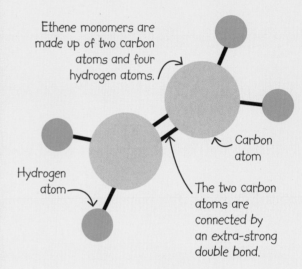

Ethene monomers are made up of two carbon atoms and four hydrogen atoms.

Carbon atom

Hydrogen atom

The two carbon atoms are connected by an extra-strong double bond.

When the double bond between each pair of carbon atoms is broken, in a process called polymerization, the ethene monomers can join together to form a chain, called a polymer.

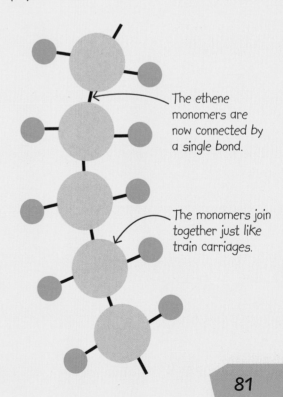

The ethene monomers are now connected by a single bond.

The monomers join together just like train carriages.

NATURAL POLYMERS

Plastic is only one type of polymer. In fact, lots of things in the natural world are made up of polymers. Silk is a natural polymer produced by animals such as the silkworm caterpillar. Rubber is made from the secretions of the rubber tree. Cellulose, found in the cell walls of plants, is used to make paper, while starch is the carbohydrate found in potatoes and our other staple foods.

Cellulose

Starch

Rubber

Silk

SYNTHETIC POLYMERS

Synthetic polymers are created by humans from chemicals, and different chemicals result in different kinds of plastics, with different uses. Plastic is brilliantly versatile and has made our lives easier in so many ways: it can be flexible enough to insulate electrical wires in our homes, or hard enough to make protective equipment on building sites. Plastic also saves lives in hospitals every day because it is cheap and hygienic.

Polystyrene
This light plastic is used to make packaging, insulation, cups and tubs, and ceiling tiles.

Polythene (also known as polyethylene)
Used for plastic bags, water bottles, food wrapping, toys, and insulation.

Polyvinyl chloride (PVC)
PVC is made into guttering and pipes, electrical insulation, flooring, and even clothes.

Nylon
Nylon is a synthetic fibre that can be made into clothes, carpets, plastic ropes, and machine parts.

Acrylic resins and fibres
Used to make paints, nail varnish, and synthetic fibres for clothing.

Beyond plastic

We use so much plastic that it has become a problem as some plastics take hundreds of years to decay. Scientists are looking for ways to replace some of the plastics we use with new materials. Some of the options include using mushroom-based packaging and switching plastic bags with alternatives made with fish scales and algae.

Pollution solution

In 2016, Japanese scientists discovered a type of bacteria that could help combat plastic pollution. These voracious eaters contain an enzyme (a substance that brings about a chemical reaction) that breaks down the plastic's molecular bonds, causing it to decompose in just six weeks.

Polyurethane (PUR)

Packaging foam, paints, varnishes, sportswear, and kitchen sponges can all be made with PUR.

Polymethyl methacrylate (PMMA)

This is a glass substitute – it's commonly called "plexiglass".

Polytetrafluoroethylene (PTFE)

This is used for waterproof clothing, machine bearings, and as a non-stick coating for cooking pots and pans.

Kevlar

High-strength materials such as bullet-proof vests are made of this plastic.

Polyester (polyethylene terephthalate, or PET)

This plastic is used to make fibreglass, synthetic fibres for clothing, and photographic film.

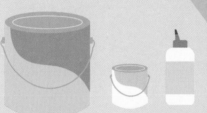

CURIOUS CHEMISTS

From mining to metalworking, humans have always experimented to find uses for the materials around them. The roots of chemistry lie in alchemy, which combined science with magic in an attempt to turn everyday metals into gold. Modern chemistry began in the 18th century, and has developed in leaps thanks to many clever scientists.

FOUR ELEMENTS

The ancient Greeks believed that everything in the Universe was made up of just four elements, an idea that influenced scientific thought for more than 2,000 years. The four elements were water, air, fire, and earth.

c. 450 BCE

c. 1st century CE

c. 3500 BCE

BRONZE AGE

The Sumerians of Mesopotamia (in modern-day Iraq) had an understanding of how metallic elements behave. They heated copper and tin together to make bronze - a hard but malleable (shapeable) metal that could be made into weapons and tools. The Sumerians also discovered the chemical process of mixing sand with soda and lime at a high temperature to make glass.

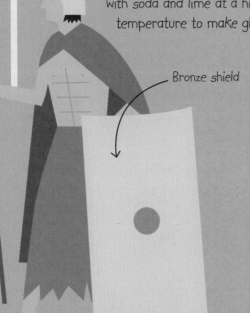

Bronze shield

MARY THE PROPHETESS

The Egyptian city of Alexandria was the alchemy centre of the ancient world. Mary the Prophetess, one of the first alchemists, is said to have invented an apparatus for distillation (purifying a substance from a solution), a version of which is still used today.

Decreasing the volume of the gas increases its pressure.

BOYLE'S LAW

Irish-born Robert Boyle is often regarded as the first modern chemist. He defined an important rule about the behaviour of gases: when the space a gas occupies decreases, the pressure of the gas increases, and vice versa. Boyle's law explains, for example, how aerosols and medical syringes work, and even what happens when we breathe.

1530

1622   1770s

CHEMICAL REVOLUTION

The French scientist Antoine Lavoisier revolutionized chemistry. He was the first person to explain accurately how combustion (the burning process) works, recognized and named the elements oxygen and hydrogen, and came up with a way of naming chemicals that we still use today. He also wrote the first modern chemistry textbook.

PARACELSUS

The Swiss alchemist Paracelsus pioneered the use of minerals and other chemicals in medical treatments. He invented remedies using mercury, sulphur, and other elements, but also recognized that some substances that can help cure people in small doses may be toxic in large quantities. He refused to rely on ancient texts, instead using his own observations. This approach influenced future chemists.

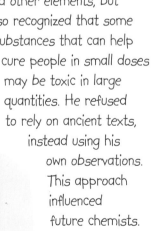

Lavoisier identified that water is two parts hydrogen and one part oxygen.

VULCANIZED RUBBER

In the 1800s, naturally occurring latex rubber had limited use in products because it cracked in cold weather and melted in the heat. By accidentally dropping some rubber mixed with sulphur on a hot stove, the American chemist Charles Goodyear discovered the vulcanization process, which makes rubber durable and weatherproof. When the motor car industry dawned a few decades later, it became the go-to material for making tyres.

BUNSEN BURNER

While studying the different kinds of light emitted by different elements as they burn, the German chemist Robert Bunsen and his colleague Peter Desaga came up with a design for a new type of economical gas burner that produced a very hot, very clean flame. Named after its inventor, the Bunsen burner is now an essential part of all chemistry labs around the world.

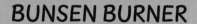

1839

1855

1812

1898

MOHS SCALE

The German geologist Friedrich Mohs invented a scale that measures a mineral's hardness. He chose 10 minerals and arranged them in order from softest to hardest, with each one able to scratch only those below it on the scale. By a simple scratch test every mineral could then be given a number on the scale. The scale helps manufacturers choose which minerals to use for their products: for example, smartphone screens use a type of hard glass that registers around 7 on the scale.

RADIUM DISCOVERED

While researching radioactivity, the Polish-French chemist Marie Curie and her French husband Pierre discovered a new light-emitting element: radium. Soon after, they discovered that it might be able to destroy cancer cells. Their work led to the development of radiotherapy, a cancer treatment using radium that now saves the lives of millions of people every year.

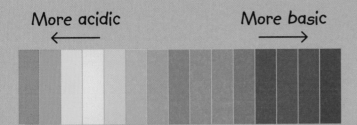

More acidic ← → More basic

PH SCALE

While studying the fermentation process at the Carlsberg Brewery in Denmark, the chemist Søren Sørensen invented the pH scale – a way to test how acidic or basic a chemical is. When acids are mixed with water, they form hydrogen ions (ions are atoms with an electric charge), and have a low pH, which stands for "potential of hydrogen". Alkaline (basic) substances have few hydrogen ions, and a high pH.

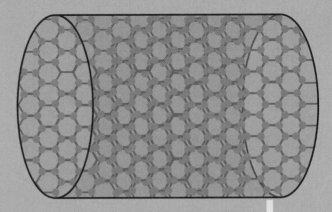

GRAPHENE

Graphene is a very strong form of carbon, only one atom thick. It is already used to make tiny, very powerful microprocessors in products such as smartphones, and it may be used in future to increase the efficiency of solar panels.

1965

Today

1909   1920s

FROZEN FOODS

Until the 1920s, frozen food was mushy and tasteless when cooked. While working in Labrador, Canada, the inventor Clarence Birdseye noticed that the local Inuit people froze the fish they caught immediately in snow. Months later, it still tasted fresh. Back in his native US, Birdseye developed a way of quick-freezing food between two metal plates at very low temperatures, which prevented ice crystals from forming and damaging the food.

KEVLAR

When carrying out experiments with polymers, the American chemist Stephanie Kwolek had a lucky hunch. Rather than throwing away a batch of a solution that had gone unexpectedly cloudy and runny, she investigated further. She found it could be spun into an incredibly tough fibre, five times stronger than steel. She named it Kevlar, and today it is used to make dozens of strong and lightweight products, from racing boats to running shoes.

Kevlar has been used in many everyday items, including trainers.

WHAT'S THE POINT OF
EARTH SCIENCE?

Imagine having no idea if a cyclone was coming or an earthquake was about to strike – life would be far more dangerous! What causes changes to Earth and its atmosphere, and piecing together how the planet has evolved over time, are questions that occupy earth scientists. Answering these can help us find solutions to the problems, such as global warming, that threaten our future on Earth.

WHY DO WE NEED EARTH SCIENCE?

If you live on Earth – and you probably do! – then Earth science is crucial to your survival. Scientists in this field are interested in our planet: from its history to the present-day condition of its air, water, and land, and how these change over time. They help to save lives by alerting us about earthquakes, typhoons, and hurricanes before they strike. And, by revealing how human activity is increasing Earth's surface temperature, they have flagged up one of the most important issues of our time: global warming.

WHAT IS EARTH SCIENCE?

Earth science is a big subject, and there are lots of different areas of study. Geologists study rocks and minerals, oceanologists are experts on the world's oceans, and meteorologists analyse weather patterns in the atmosphere. These different specialists, and many more, contribute to our understanding of our complex and fragile planet, and how we can protect it.

The Sun is essential for life on Earth. It provides the light and heat needed for living things to grow.

The atmosphere is like a big blanket that protects Earth from the Sun's heat and radiation from space.

Mountains store at least 60 per cent of the world's fresh water, much of it as ice.

Only 2 per cent of Earth's surface is covered by rainforests, but they contain half of the world's plant and animal species.

Oceans cover 70 per cent of the world's surface. The waves and tides are sources of renewable energy.

Discarded plastic often ends up in the ocean, causing harm to sea life.

Sand is tiny grains of rock that have been worn smooth by waves and wind.

Rocks are formed of one or more minerals – naturally occurring substances made from chemical elements.

WHAT IS GLOBAL WARMING?

Small amounts of certain gases in the atmosphere help trap the Sun's energy. This is called the greenhouse effect, and helps keep the planet warm. Over the last 150 years, however, human activities, such as burning coal, oil, and gas, have caused the level of these greenhouse gases in the atmosphere to rise, which in turn has caused average temperatures on Earth to increase. This is having a devastating effect on the environment, melting ice caps and glaciers, and leading to more floods, rainfall, and extreme weather events across the world.

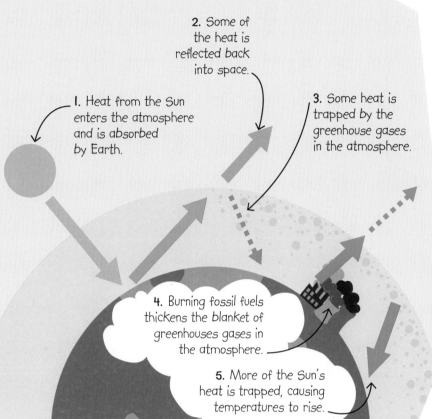

2. Some of the heat is reflected back into space.

1. Heat from the Sun enters the atmosphere and is absorbed by Earth.

3. Some heat is trapped by the greenhouse gases in the atmosphere.

4. Burning fossil fuels thickens the blanket of greenhouses gases in the atmosphere.

5. More of the Sun's heat is trapped, causing temperatures to rise.

EVERYDAY EARTH SCIENCE

An important part of Earth science is studying the impact of human activity on the environment. By identifying where humans are damaging Earth, such as by causing pollution, and developing better ways of managing the world's resources, we can live more in harmony with the planet.

Overfishing and pollution are two key areas that affect the lives of sea animals, and the health of oceans generally.

Energy can be produced by the rise and fall of ocean tides. Using this natural resource could help combat global warming.

Earth is full of natural resources, from metals to precious stones, and also resources such as coal, oil, and gas, which can be burned to produce power.

Earth science has deepened our understanding of earthquakes, which has saved lives and increased building safety in many earthquake-affected areas.

WILL IT RAIN TOMORROW?

The weather can be unpredictable, but for centuries people have tried to forecast what might happen. Whether you're planning a day out, growing crops, or need to know if a hurricane might strike, weather forecasting helps us every day. From tracking wind patterns and recording rainfall to measuring temperatures and air pressure, a lot of work goes into predicting the weather.

1 For centuries, Korean farmers measured rainfall to try to predict weather patterns. Knowing when it might rain would help them grow as many healthy crops as possible throughout the year.

2 They measured the depth of puddles to see how much rain had fallen during a downpour. Although useful, this method only offered an estimate, and wasn't very accurate.

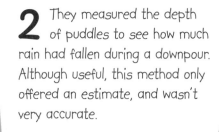

Rain gauges

Modern rain gauges work in just the same way as *cheugugis*. A rain gauge is simply a cylinder with a scale in millimetres or inches. If 25 mm (1 in) of water collects in it, then that is the recorded rainfall.

3 In 1441, at the king's request, Korean inventors built a device to measure rainfall more precisely. The *cheugugi* was an iron rain gauge, with a pipe to stop splashing.

4 Dipping a ruler into the water gave an accurate measure of rainfall. *Cheugugis* were sent all over Korea, and they enabled scientists to create detailed records about rainfall that helped farmers across the country.

93

Planning ahead

Accurate weather forecasts are still essential to farming today. If bad weather may be on the way, farmers need to know as soon as possible so they can plan ahead and protect their crops.

DRY OR DAMP?

Humidity is the amount of water vapour in the air. In ancient China, people measured humidity by measuring the weight of a piece of charcoal. In humid weather, charcoal absorbs water vapour and gets heavier. In dry weather, the water evaporates and the charcoal gets lighter. In weather terms, hot and dry days have low humidity, with cold and moist days usually having high humidity.

A known weight of charcoal was left exposed to the air.

The increase in the charcoal's weight gave a measure of humidity.

SUNNY OR STORMY?

The air in Earth's atmosphere presses on everything with a force called atmospheric pressure. High pressure is a sign of fine, sunny weather, but low pressure can mean wind, rain, and storms. In 1643, the Italian scientist Evangelista Torricelli invented the mercury barometer – the first tool that could accurately measure atmospheric pressure.

Inside the top of the glass tube is a vacuum (a space with no air).

High pressure pushes mercury up the tube. Markings on the side allow for a reading to be made.

Atmospheric pressure

The basin is filled with mercury – a metal that is liquid at room temperature.

TRY IT OUT
MAKE A RAIN GAUGE

You can make your very own *cheugugi* using an old plastic bottle. First cut the top off. Then attach a ruler to the outside or use a marker pen to copy the ruler's scale onto the outside of the bottle. Pour water into the bottle until it reaches the zero mark. Then replace the top to form a funnel. Leave your rain gauge outdoors, and record what it says after it rains.

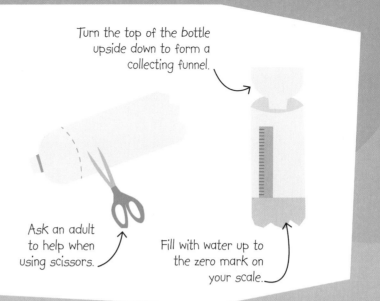

Turn the top of the bottle upside down to form a collecting funnel.

Ask an adult to help when using scissors.

Fill with water up to the zero mark on your scale.

HOT OR COLD?

Temperature is a measure of how hot or cold something is. The Polish-Dutch scientist Daniel Fahrenheit invented the mercury thermometer – the first tool that could measure temperature reliably. Mercury expands as it gets warmer and rises up the glass tube. Fahrenheit also invented the temperature scale named after him.

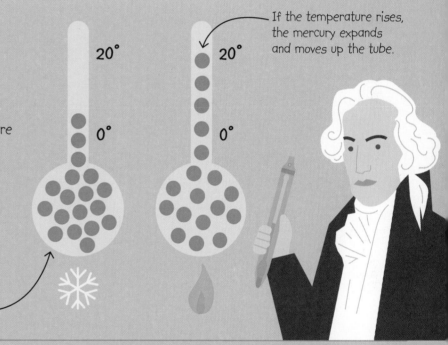

If the temperature rises, the mercury expands and moves up the tube.

If the temperature falls, the mercury contracts and moves down the tube.

WEATHER FORECAST

Weather stations and satellites orbiting Earth collect data about humidity, air pressure, temperature, rainfall, and other features of Earth's atmosphere. This data is then fed into powerful computers that run models to predict what the weather will be in the future. Modern weather forecasts can predict the weather a week in advance with about 80 per cent accuracy.

The lines are called isobars and show areas of equal atmospheric pressure.

Simple images are used to show what to expect from the weather in different places.

HOW TO KNOW WHERE YOU ARE

From the *beginning* of time, people used landmarks to figure out how to get around their local area. But if they wanted to travel further afield, they had to be able to work out where they were in order to reach their destination safely. Over time, they developed clever ways to work out their latitude (how far north or south they were) and longitude (how far east or west they were).

1 People across the world figured out that a good way of measuring their latitude was to look at the night sky. While most stars appear to move each night, Polaris (also called the North Star) seems to stay in the same position. Its height in the sky depends on your position on Earth.

Polaris is part of the Ursa Minor constellation.

The angle between Polaris and the horizon gave the traveller their latitude.

Line of sight

3 They would then hold the piece of wood in front of them, lining it up so the bottom edge was level with the horizon and the top edge was level with Polaris. They tied a knot in the string to record their position.

Knot

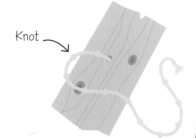

2 Around 900 CE, Arab explorers developed a simple device called a *kamal* to work out their position. Before leaving home, the traveller would tie a knot in a piece of string, thread it through a small piece of wood so the knot stops the string from slipping through, and hold the string taut using their teeth.

Polaris and latitude

Polaris is useful for finding latitude *because* it sits directly above the North Pole. Because of this, it doesn't change position as Earth rotates on its axis. If you're at the equator (written as 0°), it sits on the horizon and gets higher as you go north, until it's directly overhead (90°N) at the North Pole. Unfortunately, this method did not work for travellers south of the equator as there isn't a star in the southern night sky like Polaris.

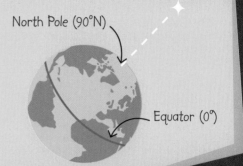

North Pole (90°N)

Equator (0°)

In the traveller's new position, Polaris is higher in the sky, which means they have moved north.

4 When the traveller reached a new destination, they would use the *kamal* to take a new reading of the position of Polaris in the sky by moving the wooden board closer to or further away from their face. They would tie a new knot to mark their new position.

5 Travellers would make many knots in their *kamal* to mark important places. If they got lost, they could use their *kamal* to work out which place they'd previously recorded they were close to. It wouldn't show them how to get there, but they would know that they were to the east or west of something they recognized.

REAL WORLD

The sextant

In time, travellers developed more advanced ways of working out latitude. The marine sextant could accurately measure the angle between the horizon and the Sun and stars against a scale, allowing travellers to pinpoint their positions with greater precision.

HOW LONGITUDE WAS WORKED OUT

By the 18th century, trade across the world's oceans was increasing dramatically. But sailors had a problem. Without knowing their longitude it was easy to get lost at sea, which often led to shipwrecks. Great scientists such as Galileo Galilei and Edmond Halley had looked to the stars to solve the problem of longitude, but then in 1728 the English watchmaker John Harrison hit upon the answer: he realized it was far easier to use a clock.

1 Harrison knew that as Earth is a rotating sphere, it spins 360° in one day. There are 24 hours in a day, which means every hour it rotates 15°. This explains why different places on the globe have different times.

$$360° / 24 = 15°$$

2 But how could a ship in the middle of the ocean work out its longitude? The answer lay in measuring time. A sailor could tell when it was noon wherever they were as it was when the Sun was highest in the sky. If they also knew what the time was at a reference point, (the time in London, England was the one most used), they could roughly work out their longitude by comparing the two.

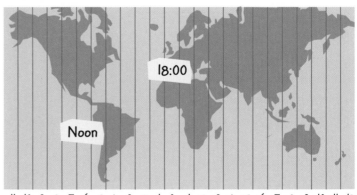

18:00

Noon

-11 -10 -9 -8 -7 -6 -5 -4 -3 -2 -1 0 +1 +2 +3 +4 +5 +6 +7 +8 +9 +10 +11 +12

REAL WORLD

Global Positioning System
We now use a network of satellites on the ground and in orbit around Earth – plus some complex maths – to know exactly where we are. Called the Global Positioning System (GPS), the satellites in space send signals to a GPS device (such as a smartphone). The device then uses maths to work out where it is on Earth correct to a few metres.

3 Harrison's mission was to build a sea clock that would not lose or gain time due to changes in temperature and a ship's constant motion – so that when the sailors used it on the oceans, they would be confident that the comparison between the two times would be accurate.

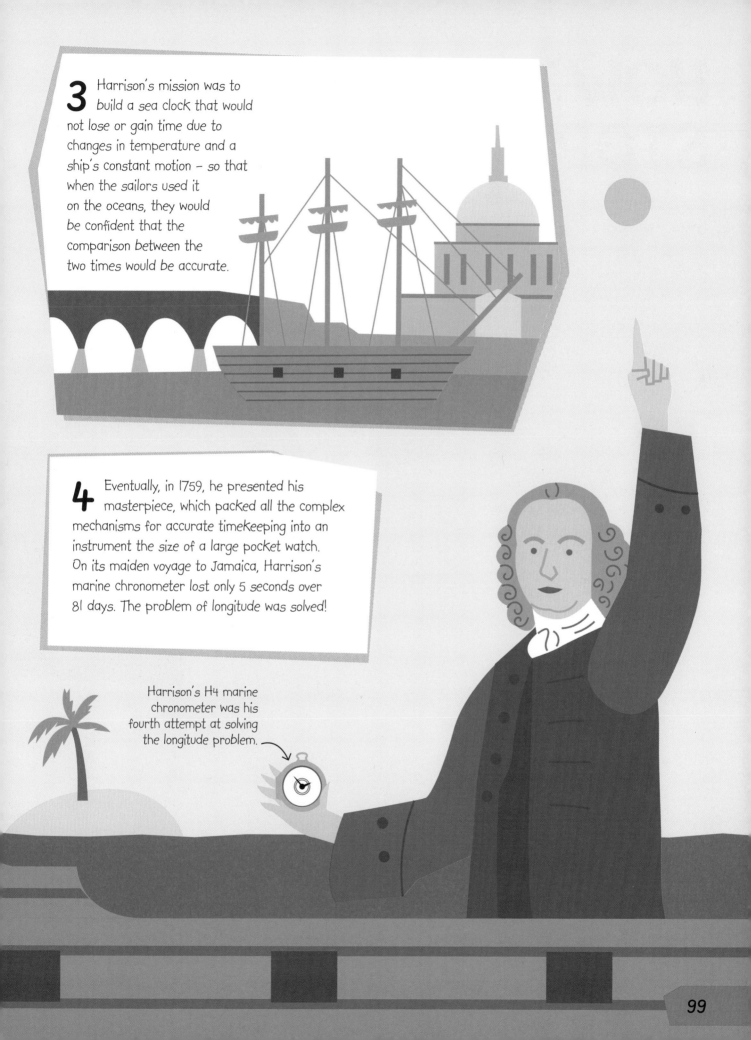

4 Eventually, in 1759, he presented his masterpiece, which packed all the complex mechanisms for accurate timekeeping into an instrument the size of a large pocket watch. On its maiden voyage to Jamaica, Harrison's marine chronometer lost only 5 seconds over 81 days. The problem of longitude was solved!

Harrison's H4 marine chronometer was his fourth attempt at solving the longitude problem.

HOW TO STOP A BOMB

Most atoms are stable, but a few rare types are radioactive, which means they can break apart and release dangerous forms of radiation. Radioactive materials are used to treat cancer and generate electricity, but they can also cause deadly pollution. In the 1950s, when more and more nuclear weapons were being tested in seemingly remote corners of the globe, a Japanese scientist realized that their radioactive leftovers were on the verge of poisoning the entire Pacific Ocean.

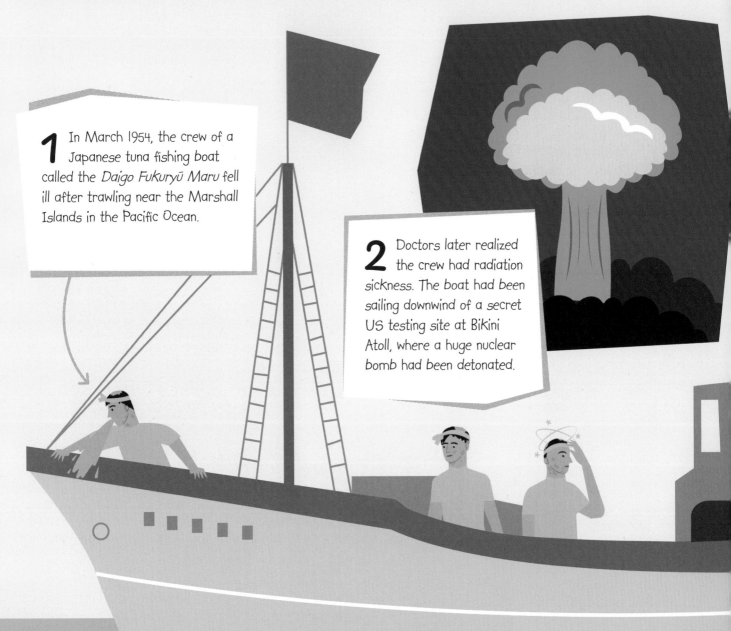

1 In March 1954, the crew of a Japanese tuna fishing boat called the *Daigo Fukuryū Maru* fell ill after trawling near the Marshall Islands in the Pacific Ocean.

2 Doctors later realized the crew had radiation sickness. The boat had been sailing downwind of a secret US testing site at Bikini Atoll, where a huge nuclear bomb had been detonated.

3 The Japanese government asked the scientist Katsuko Saruhashi to investigate how fallout (radioactive pollution) from the bomb had travelled around the Pacific Ocean. She discovered that ocean currents carried the fallout clockwise, concentrating it in certain areas. She also realized that if nobody did anything about it, many of the animals in the Pacific Ocean would eventually become contaminated or die out completely.

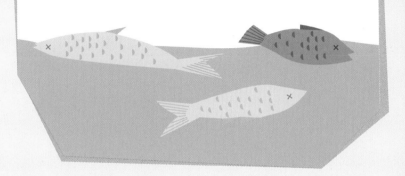

4 Saruhashi's work caused an international incident, and the US had to admit that it had been testing nuclear weapons in the Pacific Ocean. Soon after, the US and other countries agreed to stop testing nuclear bombs underwater, in the atmosphere, and in space.

Understanding the science
NUCLEAR RADIATION

If an atom is unstable, its nucleus can break apart (decay) at any moment. When a nucleus decays, it releases large amounts of energy as nuclear radiation. This radiation may take the form of fast-moving particles (such as alpha particles) or waves travelling at the speed of light.

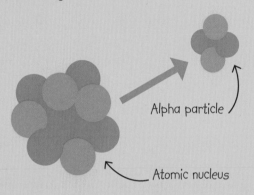

Alpha particle

Atomic nucleus

There are three main types of nuclear radiation: alpha, beta, and gamma radiation. Alpha radiation has the least penetrating power – even skin can block it. Gamma radiation is more penetrating and passes easily through the human body.

Beta radiation can pass through skin but can be blocked by a thin sheet of metal.

Alpha

Beta

Gamma

Alpha radiation can be stopped by skin.

A thick layer of lead is needed to block gamma radiation.

NUCLEAR WEAPONS

Nuclear bombs are the world's most devastating weapons and have only been used twice in war. They work either by splitting atomic nuclei (nuclear fission) or by forcing atomic nuclei together (fusion). Either way, vast amounts of energy are released, giving these bombs enormous explosive power. Fusion bombs are more powerful and destructive than fission bombs, but fission bombs produce far more radioactive fallout.

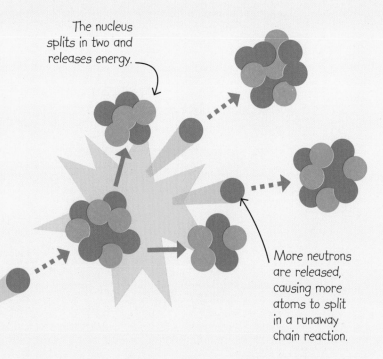

The nucleus splits in two and releases energy.

In a fission bomb, neutron particles collide with unstable uranium nuclei, which makes them split.

More neutrons are released, causing more atoms to split in a runaway chain reaction.

NUCLEAR ENERGY

Nuclear power stations use the heat released by nuclear fission to generate electricity. Unlike nuclear bombs, power stations keep fission reactions under control by separating rods of nuclear fuel with materials that absorb neutrons. Nuclear energy has advantages and disadvantages. It doesn't produce greenhouse gases such as carbon dioxide, but the waste from a nuclear reactor stays radioactive for thousands of years, and has to be buried deep underground.

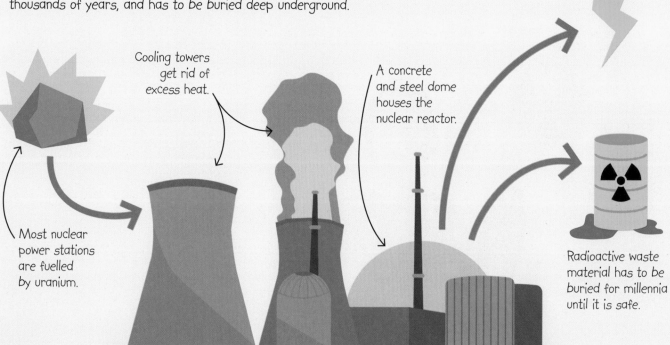

Heat from the reaction drives generators, which make electricity.

Cooling towers get rid of excess heat.

A concrete and steel dome houses the nuclear reactor.

Most nuclear power stations are fuelled by uranium.

Radioactive waste material has to be buried for millennia until it is safe.

RADIOTHERAPY

Nuclear radiation can cause cancer, but it can also be used to treat it. This treatment, known as radiotherapy, damages the DNA in cancer cells so that they can't divide or grow any more. During a treatment session, multiple beams of gamma radiation are aimed at the person's body so that they all intersect at the tumour (cancerous growth). This gives the tumour a large dose of radiation but exposes the surrounding healthy areas to just one beam each. Radiotherapy can damage some of the patient's healthy cells, but this is considered a worthwhile risk.

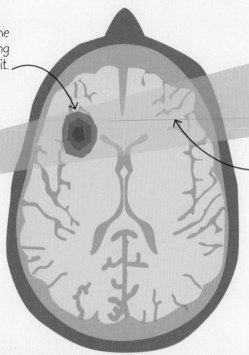

Gamma rays are aimed at the tumour from many directions.

Every beam strikes the tumour, damaging the cancer cells inside it.

Some healthy cells are also damaged, making the patient feel unwell.

REAL WORLD

Coral bleaching
As well as helping save the Pacific from radioactivity, Katsuko Saruhashi was one of the first scientists to measure carbon dioxide levels in sea water. We now know that rising carbon dioxide levels have made sea water more acidic. This is one of the reasons coral reefs have bleached (turned white) and died in many places.

EXCELLENT EARTH SCIENTISTS

Earth hasn't always looked the way it does today, and nor will it in the future. Likewise, our understanding of why changes to our unique planet take place – from what causes mountains and oceans to form, to being able to forecast tomorrow's weather – has evolved over many centuries.

EARTHQUAKE!

The Chinese scientist Zhang Heng invented the world's first device to detect earthquakes. It had eight moving arms shaped as dragon heads at each point of the compass, with eight frog-shaped containers beneath. Shock waves triggered a pendulum, causing a ball to drop into the mouth of one of the frogs, indicating the earthquake's direction.

Each dragon holds a ball in its mouth.

An earthquake causes a pendulum to swing, opening the dragon's jaw.

The ball drops into the frog's mouth.

132 CE

c. 350 BCE

Precipitation

Condensation

Evaporation

c. 1000

MOVING MOUNTAINS

While studying the mountains of Central Asia, the Arab thinker Ibn Sina speculated about how they were formed. He suggested they could be caused either by earthquakes, which suddenly forced land up from the sea bed, or the slower process of erosion, which could whittle away rock, creating valleys. On both counts, Ibn Sina was right.

WHY IT RAINS

The Greek philosopher Aristotle is believed to be the first person to figure out what causes rain. He argued correctly that the Sun's heat causes water to evaporate into water vapour and rise to the upper atmosphere. The cold then causes it to condense and fall again as precipitation (rain or snow).

TEMPERATURE GAUGE

Soon after Daniel Fahrenheit's invention of the thermometer, the Swedish astronomer Anders Celsius devised a new temperature scale. Celsius had been working on experiments around the freezing and boiling points of water and wanted a scale with measurements between these two points. He called it "centigrade" (after the Latin for "100 steps"). Some 200 years later, the scientific community renamed the scale after its creator.

On the original centigrade scale, water's boiling point was at 0°C and its freezing point was at 100°C, but the values were soon flipped around.

OLDER EARTH

Influenced by the Bible, many people believed that Earth was only a few thousand years old. A French naturalist, Comte de Buffon, argued that the existence of fossils meant that it could be far older – perhaps millions of years. He underestimated Earth's real age but his non-biblical explanation of natural history was revolutionary for the time, and opened up a long debate.

1749

1742

1088

FOSSILIZED RECORDS

The Chinese scientist Shen Kuo was one of the first people to come up with a theory of climate change. A landslide near his home in Yanzhou revealed a forest of fossilized bamboo shoots that had turned to stone. Shen Kuo knew that bamboo couldn't live in such a dry climate. This led him to the conclusion that conditions in Yanzhou must have been very different in the past and to a groundbreaking theory: that it was possible for the climate to change.

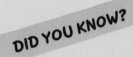

DID YOU KNOW?

Rival theories

In the late 18th century, the scientific world was bitterly divided over two theories. Some thought that changes to Earth's surface only happened through natural disasters such as floods. Others argued that natural processes occurred over long periods of time. These ideas won through, and were a major influence on the work of Charles Darwin.

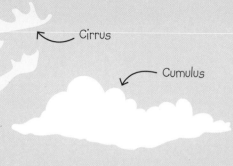

Cirrus

Cumulus

Stratus

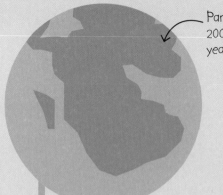

Pangea about 200 million years ago

UP IN THE CLOUDS

Before the 19th century, scientists hadn't given much thought to clouds. But they were a passion for English amateur weather watcher, Luke Howard, who spent his time sketching them. The patterns he spotted inspired him to classify them into three main types. In time, more names were added to describe the combinations of these types.

PANGEA

The German scientist Alfred Wegener put forward the idea that between 335 and 175 million years ago, all of the modern-day continents had formed a single landmass called Pangea. A process called continental drift had caused the continent to break apart. His theory may explain why similar animals are found on opposite sides of the world.

1802   1846   1912

1913

SEISMIC WAVES

The Irish scientist Robert Mallet came up with a solution to a question that had long puzzled scientists: what causes earthquakes? He realized that they are the result of movements of rocks underground. These cause vibrations that travel up to Earth's surface. He called these "seismic waves".

DATING ROCKS

By studying the rate at which the element uranium had decayed into lead in a piece of rock, the English geologist Arthur Holmes worked out that Earth was at least 1.6 billion years old. His work led scientists to establish Earth's true age in the 1950s: 4.6 billion years old.

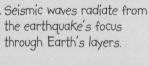

Seismic waves radiate from the earthquake's focus through Earth's layers.

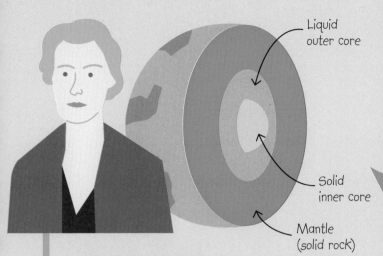

Liquid outer core

Solid inner core

Mantle (solid rock)

EXTINCTION EVENT

What happened to the dinosaurs? The American physicist Luis Walter Alvarez and his son, Walter, found evidence that 66 million years ago an asteroid 9 km (5.6 miles) wide slammed into the Gulf of Mexico, causing earthquakes and tsunamis, and spreading debris that blocked out sunlight for more than a year. The resulting death of plants may have led to the starvation of the dinosaurs.

SOLID CORE

Scientists used to believe that Earth's metallic core was liquid. While studying the seismic waves caused by earthquakes, the Danish seismologist Inge Lehmann realized that Earth's spherical centre is in fact made up of two layers: a liquid outer core and, at the very centre, a previously undiscovered inner core made up of solid iron and nickel.

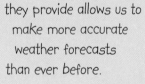

1980

Today

1936   1962

ENVIRONMENTAL CONCERNS

Rachel Carson, an American biologist, discovered that heavy use of pesticides in modern farming was polluting soils and streams, and causing birds and other animals to die. She published an influential book, *Silent Spring*, which drew attention to the damage humans do to the environment. Her work is now regarded as having kickstarted the environmental movement.

SATELLITE SAVIOURS

Satellites orbit Earth providing information about our planet that wouldn't be possible from the ground. They help us to find out the effects of climate change by measuring changes in the gases in Earth's atmosphere such as ozone and carbon dioxide. The images they beam back give us information on climate emergencies, such as the spread of wildfires and the shrinking ice caps. And the data they provide allows us to make more accurate weather forecasts than ever before.

WHAT'S THE POINT OF
SPACE SCIENCE?

Space science constantly pushes the boundaries of what is believed to be possible. A century ago, few people thought humans would ever set foot on the Moon. Today, we have robots on Mars, and are planning to have humans there soon, too. Scientists are even edging ever closer to answering one of the biggest questions of all: are we alone in the Universe?

WHY DO WE NEED SPACE SCIENCE?

How did the Universe begin? How will it end? Could life exist beyond our world? These are huge questions, and they're ones that space scientists study. It's an exciting, fast-changing subject. Each year, space science reveals more and more about the wider Universe. And along the way, it has brought us new inventions and technologies, from satellites to safety equipment, that have changed our world.

WHAT IS SPACE SCIENCE?

Space science explores the Universe – the largest laboratory ever! It's a subject that's both very old and very new. Our early ancestors tracked the phases of the Moon to create the first calendars, and medieval astronomers studied the orbits of the planets. Today, space science brings together all the sciences – physics, chemistry, biology, computer science, engineering, even maths – with the purpose of figuring out how the Universe works, and our place within it.

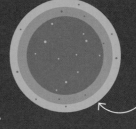

A comet is a big lump of gas and dirty ice that orbits the Sun.

The Sun's light sustains life on Earth, and our planet orbits around it.

An asteroid is a chunk of rock or metal. Like comets, asteroids orbit the Sun.

WHAT'S THE POINT OF LIGHT-YEARS?

Distances in space are so vast that we use special units called light-years to measure them. A light-year is the distance light travels in one year. That's about 9.5 trillion km (5.9 trillion miles)! Because objects in space are so far away, it takes a long time for their light to reach Earth.

Earth is about 8.3 light-minutes from the Sun, our closest star.

It is about 4.3 light-years from Proxima Centauri, our next closest star.

It is about 323 light-years from Polaris, also known as the North Star.

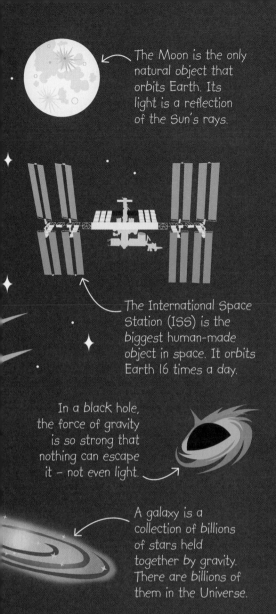

The Moon is the only natural object that orbits Earth. Its light is a reflection of the Sun's rays.

The International Space Station (ISS) is the biggest human-made object in space. It orbits Earth 16 times a day.

In a black hole, the force of gravity is so strong that nothing can escape it – not even light.

A galaxy is a collection of billions of stars held together by gravity. There are billions of them in the Universe.

Space probes travel beyond Earth's orbit far into outer space. They don't carry a crew.

EVERYDAY SPACE SCIENCE

Space is a very hostile place, with extreme temperatures, no oxygen, and the risk of radiation. It has taken a vast amount of research by some very clever people to make space exploration possible. This research has led to the development of all sorts of amazing new inventions, many of which we now use to benefit our daily lives here on Earth.

Technology developed by NASA (the US space agency) to make drinking water for crews in space is now used to purify water in the developing world.

The need to make small and powerful computers for space missions led to the lightweight laptops and handheld devices many of us use today.

Fabrics created for space suits are now used to make heat-resistant, flameproof protective clothing for firefighters.

The tiny digital cameras on our mobile phones are all thanks to NASA, who developed a way of making cameras much smaller without losing image quality.

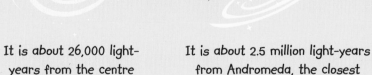

It is about 26,000 light-years from the centre of the Milky Way.

It is about 2.5 million light-years from Andromeda, the closest galaxy to the Milky Way.

It's about 13.4 billion light-years away from the most distant galaxy we know of, called GN-z11.

HOW TO DEFY GRAVITY

The first rockets – fireworks invented around 1000 CE in China – were able to reach high in the sky. But it wasn't until the 20th century that scientists developed a rocket powerful enough to be launched into outer space. This breakthrough made it possible for humankind to discover more about our Solar System, and beyond, than anyone could ever have dreamed.

1 In 1903, Russian scientist Konstantin Tsiolkovsky published his "rocket equation". His calculations showed how a rocket powered by liquid fuel could theoretically be made to accelerate fast enough to escape Earth's gravity and reach orbit.

$$\triangle v = v_e \ln \frac{m_0}{}$$

2 In 1926, American scientist Robert Goddard launched the first liquid-fuelled rocket. Powered by igniting petrol and liquid oxygen, it shot 12.5 m (41 ft) into the air before crashing back down to Earth two seconds later.

Understanding the science
ESCAPE VELOCITY

Earth's gravity pulls everything on it and around the planet towards it. In order to overcome this gravitational pull, an object has to move extremely fast. This is known as "escape velocity". Rockets have to burn a lot of fuel to reach these mind-boggling speeds.

Back to Earth
Anything – from a tennis ball to a spacecraft – that doesn't travel fast enough will be pulled back to Earth by the planet's gravitational pull.

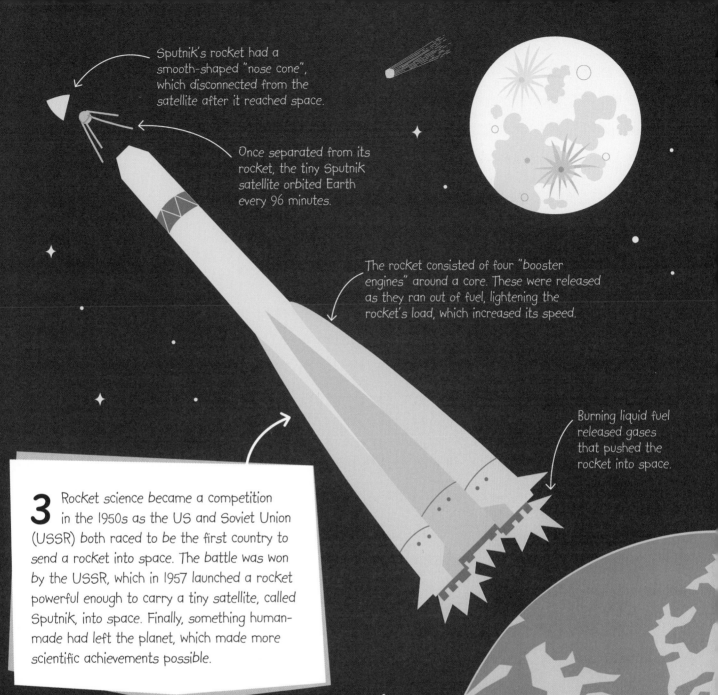

Sputnik's rocket had a smooth-shaped "nose cone", which disconnected from the satellite after it reached space.

Once separated from its rocket, the tiny Sputnik satellite orbited Earth every 96 minutes.

The rocket consisted of four "booster engines" around a core. These were released as they ran out of fuel, lightening the rocket's load, which increased its speed.

Burning liquid fuel released gases that pushed the rocket into space.

3 Rocket science became a competition in the 1950s as the US and Soviet Union (USSR) both raced to be the first country to send a rocket into space. The battle was won by the USSR, which in 1957 launched a rocket powerful enough to carry a tiny satellite, called Sputnik, into space. Finally, something human-made had left the planet, which made more scientific achievements possible.

Orbiting Earth
If a spacecraft travels at 27,000 km/h (17,000 mph) it will enter space, but will be balanced by Earth's gravitational pull. This results in the craft orbiting the planet, as Sputnik did.

Escaping orbit
If it travels faster than 40,000 km/h (25,000 mph), a spacecraft will escape Earth's gravitational pull and travel out into the Solar System.

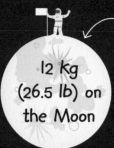

The Moon is the only other Solar System object that humans have stood on, besides Earth.

12 kg (26.5 lb) on the Moon

26.5 kg (58.5 lb) on Mercury

27.5 kg (60 lb) on Mars

65 kg (143 lb) on Uranus

GRAVITY, MASS, AND WEIGHT

Everything has gravity, but only massive objects like planets and stars have enough gravity to significantly affect other objects. Mass is the amount of matter in an object. The more mass an object has, the stronger its gravitational pull. Weight is the measure of how strongly gravity pulls on mass. This is the reason why an astronaut would weigh different amounts in different places in the Solar System – the more massive a planet is, the stronger the planet's gravitational pull will be, which increases an astronaut's weight if they stand on that planet.

The astronaut has the same mass always, but would have different weights if they stood on different Solar System objects.

66 kg (145.5 lb) on Venus

73 kg (161 lb) on Earth

77.5 kg (171 lb) on Saturn

82 kg (181 lb) on Neptune

DID YOU KNOW?

What does gravity do?
Earth's gravity is what causes a ball to drop when we throw it – gravity pulls the ball towards Earth's centre. It's also gravity that keeps our feet on the ground, and holds the Moon in orbit around Earth.

Jupiter is the most massive planet in the Solar System, so it pulls on objects around and on it more.

184.5 kg (407 lb) on Jupiter

SPACE CURVES

Scientists still aren't sure what causes gravity, but Albert Einstein's theory is that gravity is caused by "curves" in space. His theory of general relativity suggests that large objects create a curve or dip, which other nearby objects are pulled into. Larger objects create bigger curves, which makes their gravitational pull stronger.

A star creates a huge curve in space that can pull in many planets.

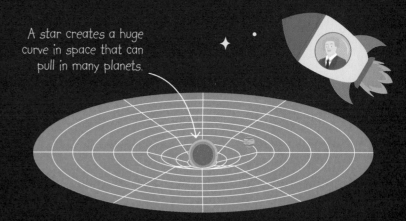

GRAVITY ASSIST

Spacecraft only have a limited amount of fuel, and one way space scientists conserve this is by using gravity, in what scientists call a "gravity assist". When a spacecraft passes close to a planet, it can use the planet's gravitational pull to help it speed up or slow down, without using up precious fuel.

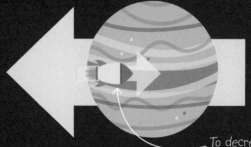

To decrease speed, the spacecraft travels against the direction of the planet's rotation.

The craft can then leave the planet's orbit on a different trajectory, and with more speed.

As a spacecraft gets closer to a planet, it begins to feel the planet's gravitational pull.

Now within the planet's orbit, the spacecraft receives momentum from the planet's rotation, and saves fuel.

REAL WORLD

Juno mission

In 2013, two years into its journey to Jupiter, NASA's *Juno* spacecraft used a gravity assist to swing around Earth. The boost it received was almost as powerful as the spacecraft's original rocket launch. It reached Jupiter in 2016.

HOW DID IT ALL BEGIN?

In the mid-20th century, scientists disagreed about how the Universe began. One group believed that the Universe had always existed and always would, whereas another group thought it exploded into existence after a "Big Bang". The two groups were at loggerheads until two scientists stumbled on an unbelievable discovery.

1 In 1964, the American scientists Arno Penzias and Robert Wilson were using a giant antenna in Holmdel, New Jersey, US, to investigate radio signals coming from our galaxy, the Milky Way. They noticed a strange background hum, which sounded like radio static.

2 Wherever they pointed the antenna, even at areas of empty space, it still picked up the sound. A family of pigeons had set up home inside the antenna. Perhaps pigeon poo was causing interference, they wondered? So they removed the nest and cleared out the poo. But still the noise persisted.

3 Still puzzled, the men discovered an intriguing theory by a fellow scientist, Robert Dicke, and invited him to listen. Together, they realized something incredible: that the humming sound was actually leftover radiation from the beginning of the Universe – the Big Bang!

Understanding the science
COSMIC MICROWAVE BACKGROUND RADIATION

The leftover radiation the giant antenna picked up is known as cosmic microwave background (CMB) radiation. Astronomers believe that the CMB is the glow left after the Big Bang. Its discovery supported Robert Dicke's theory that if the Big Bang had happened, the huge initial explosion would have left trace amounts of heat radiation throughout the Universe.

This image shows variations in the temperature of the CMB across the Universe.

Red areas represent warmer-than-average areas, and blue areas are colder than average.

HOW DID EVERYTHING START?

According to the Big Bang theory, the Universe began 13.8 billion years ago. Everything in it was compacted into a single, tiny speck. A huge explosion – the Big Bang – caused this to rapidly expand in an instant, bringing the Universe that we know into existence. It has carried on expanding ever since.

The CMB, the glow left over from the Big Bang, dates back to this time.

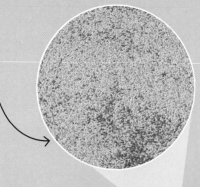

Big Bang

The Big Bang got the expansion of the Universe started.

Universe grows

In a fraction of a second, the Universe expanded vastly.

Matter is created

As the Universe expanded, it started to cool. Matter – what everything is made of – started to form.

Particles form

After about a second, the subatomic particles protons and neutrons formed.

Atoms form

After about 380,000 years, electrons and neutrons combined to form the first atoms.

OUR PLACE IN THE UNIVERSE

Our Sun is one of at least 100 billion stars that form a galaxy called the Milky Way. Galaxies have different shapes – the Milky Way is a spiral galaxy with several "arms" that swirl out from the centre. Our Solar System is located on a minor arm, called the Orion Arm.

Earth is the third planet from the Sun.

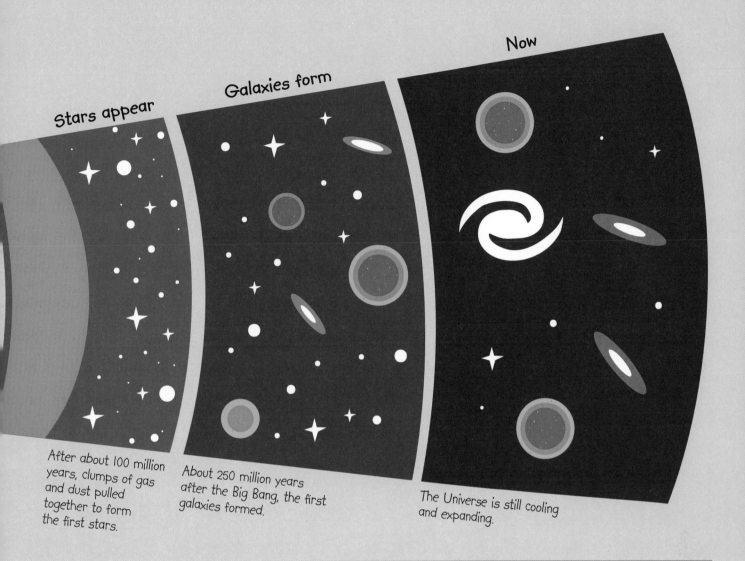

Stars appear

Galaxies form

Now

After about 100 million years, clumps of gas and dust pulled together to form the first stars.

About 250 million years after the Big Bang, the first galaxies formed.

The Universe is still cooling and expanding.

DID YOU KNOW?

Getting further away

The Universe is still rapidly expanding, with everything moving away from everything else at an ever-increasing rate. There might come a time, millions of years in the future, when distant stars will have moved so far away from Earth that their light will never reach it.

HOW MIGHT EVERYTHING END?

It is possible that the expansion of the Universe will eventually run out of energy, and begin to collapse back in on itself. This is known as the Big Crunch theory. It's also possible that another Universe will be born from the tiny, dense speck of matter left over after the Big Crunch.

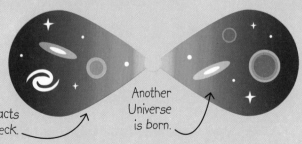

The Universe contracts into a small speck.

Another Universe is born.

SUPER SPACE SCIENTISTS

Since ancient times, humans have looked up to the skies and wondered what lies beyond our own world. From mapping the stars to sending satellites out into orbit, learning more about space has increased our knowledge of other worlds, and pushed the boundaries of what we have believed to be possible.

MAP OF THE STARS

Korean astronomers created the Cheonsang Yeolcha Bunyajido, a detailed chart that mapped the night sky. The chart shows 1,467 different stars and identifies 283 constellations – imagined patterns made by drawing lines between stars.

1395

7th century CE

1420s

KOREAN OBSERVATORY

In Gyeongju, the capital of the Silla Kingdom in modern-day Korea, astronomers built an observatory known as the Cheomseongdae. Its name means "star-gazing platform", and it helped ancient astronomers get a better look at the night's sky. The Cheomseongdae is one of the oldest observatories in the world still standing today.

The tower is made from 365 stones – one for each day of the year.

ULUGH BEG

The astronomer Ulugh Beg, who was also ruler of the Central Asian Timurid Empire, built a three-storey observatory in Samarkand (in modern-day Uzbekistan). It was destroyed in 1449, but part of a vast sextant (a tool used for calculating the position of stars) still remains.

TAQI AL-DIN OBSERVATORY

The mathematician and astronomer Taqi al-Dīn founded an observatory in the capital city of the Ottoman Empire, Constantinople (modern-day Istanbul). Although the observatory only stood for a few years, it is thought to have been one of the largest in the world at the time.

ELLIPSE

The German mathematician and astronomer Johannes Kepler pub his laws of planetary motion. The that planets move around the Su an oval path called an ellipse, an provided ways to calculate their at various points during each orb

1609

16

1577

1543

MOONS OF JUPITER

Using a telescope, the Italian astronomer Galileo Galilei discovered four moons orbiting the planet Jupiter. This showed that not everything in the Universe orbited Earth, just as Copernicus had said, and led Galileo to support Copernicus's heliocentric theory.

Galileo was one of the first scientists to make astronomical observations using a telescope.

ORBITING THE SUN

The Polish astronomer Nicolaus Copernicus published his "heliocentric" theory – that the Sun, and not Earth, lies at the centre of the Universe, and that all the planets and stars orbit around it. Although we now know that the Sun is at the centre of the Solar System, not the entire Universe, his theory was still revolutionary because it challenged the widely held beliefs of the time.

PULSATING STARS

While studying a group of stars called Cepheid variables, which "pulsate" (vary in brightness over time), the American astronomer Henrietta Swan Leavitt discovered a link between how long it took them to complete a cycle of brightness and how bright they were. This discovery made it possible to calculate these stars' distance from Earth.

BLACK HOLE DISCOVERY

For decades scientists had suspected the existence of black holes – areas of space with an incredibly strong, inescapable gravitational pull. The discovery of Cygnus X-1 during a rocket flight proved they were right. It is now recognized as a "stellar-mass black hole", meaning that it formed after a massive star collapsed in on itself.

1912   1961   1964   1967

FIRST IN SPACE

The Soviet cosmonaut Yuri Gagarin made history when he became the first person to enter space. Travelling in a space capsule called *Vostok 1*, Gagarin orbited Earth in a flight that lasted 108 minutes. After re-entering the atmosphere, he ejected from the capsule and floated back to Earth by parachute.

MYSTERY SOLVED

Using a huge telescope she had helped build, the Northern Irish physicist Jocelyn Bell Burnell detected mystery radio pulses coming from space. She and her team later worked out that they came from neutron stars – the extremely dense, collapsed remains of supergiant stars. They spin rapidly, emitting radiation. These are now known as "pulsars".

Voyager's antenna sends data back to Earth, billions of kilometres away.

HUBBLE TELESCOPE

NASA launched the Hubble Telescope into orbit – the first to be placed in space. Hubble's position above Earth's atmosphere means that it gets a much clearer view of the Universe than is possible from the surface. It has allowed scientists to peer billions of light-years into space – finding new planets, stars, galaxies, and many other phenomena.

VOYAGER 1

Launched by NASA in 1977, the *Voyager 1* space probe was sent into space to fly past Jupiter and Saturn and collect information about them. But its journey didn't stop there – in August 2012, it entered interstellar space, making it the first human-made object to leave our Solar System.

2012

2021

1969 1990

MARS MISSION

NASA's *Perseverance* rover landed on Mars with a mission to collect rock and dust samples, look for signs that life may once have existed on the planet, and test if it's possible to produce oxygen from Mars's atmosphere. Scientists have designed these tests to help prepare for future missions, which might take the first humans to the Red Planet.

FIRST MOON LANDING

Eight years after Yuri Gagarin's space flight, the American astronaut Neil Armstrong became the first person to walk on the Moon. He was followed 19 minutes later by crewmate Buzz Aldrin. While on the surface, they planted a US flag, took photos, gathered samples of lunar rock and soil, and carried out scientific experiments, before safely making their way back to Earth.

SCIENCE STARS

From mathematicians to microbiologists and astrophysicists to electrical engineers, scientists from across the globe have furthered our understanding of the world and the Universe beyond. The stars of science we've gathered here are just a few of the brilliant people we have to thank.

PHYSICS

JACK KILBY

American electrical engineer Jack Kilby (1923–2005) created the first integrated circuit (IC), or microchip. His brilliant invention meant that electronics could be made smaller, cheaper, and more reliable.

BIOLOGY

ROSALIND FRANKLIN

The British scientist Rosalind Franklin (1920–1958) made a critical contribution to our understanding of DNA, the chemical code inside the cells of living things. She took X-rays of DNA molecules that revealed their structure. This work led scientists to understand how living things pass on genetic information.

JEAN-JACQUES MUYEMBE-TAMFUM

In the 1970s, the Congolese microbiologist Jean-Jacques Muyembe-Tamfum (b. 1942) was one of the first people to identify the deadly disease Ebola. In the 2010s, he led a team that developed a successful treatment.

EARTH SCIENCE

EUNICE NEWTON FOOTE

While carrying out experiments on how the Sun's rays affect different gases, American scientist Eunice Newton Foote (1819–1888) discovered the threat posed by an increase of carbon dioxide in Earth's atmosphere. She had identified the cause of global warming.

CHEMISTRY

PERCY LAVON JULIAN

Percy Julian (1899–1975) battled racial prejudice to become one of the US's most influential chemists. He pioneered a way of chemically producing medicines from plants, making them easy to mass-produce.

JAGADISH CHANDRA BOSE

The Indian scientist Jagadish Chandra Bose (1858-1937) built a device that could detect radio signals. He chose not to patent it, which allowed Italian Guglielmo Marconi to gain fame for inventing radio instead.

NERGIS MAVALVALA

The Pakistan-born astrophysicist Nergis Mavalvala (b. 1968) was a leading member of a team that first detected gravitational waves – ripples in space caused by violent events in the Universe. Their research confirmed a major part of Albert Einstein's general theory of relativity.

MARIO J. MOLINA

The Mexican chemist Mario Molina (1943-2020) discovered that harmful human-made chemicals were damaging the ozone in Earth's atmosphere. He later helped craft a global treaty that banned these chemicals, which helped the ozone layer to heal.

WANGARI MAATHAI

The Kenyan environmentalist Wangari Maathai (1940-2011) founded the Green Belt Movement, an organization that has arranged the planting of more than 50 million trees, helping to reverse environmental destruction.

SPACE SCIENCE

VALENTINA TERESHKOVA

In 1963, the Russian cosmonaut Valentina Tereshkova (b. 1937) became the first woman to fly in space. During her mission, she did various tests to record how the human body deals with spaceflight.

SUBRAHMANYAN CHANDRASEKHAR

In the 1930s, the Indian astrophysicist Subrahmanyan Chandrasekhar (1910-1995) worked out a calculation that proved that black holes existed. It took another 40 years for the scientific world to accept his explanation.

GERTRUDE B. ELION

While researching new medicines, American chemist Gertrude B. Elion (1908-1999) developed a method of designing drugs so that they targeted the germs causing disease within cells without harming the cells themselves. Her research led to successful treatments for leukaemia, malaria, and several viral infections.

GLOSSARY

ACID
A substance with a pH value of less than 7.

ALCHEMY
An early form of chemistry, in which scholars attempted to find an elusive substance called the "philosopher's stone". They thought this could transform ordinary metals into gold.

ALLELE
A version of a gene that comes in several different variants.

ANTIBIOTIC
A medicine that kills bacteria.

ATOMS
Tiny particles that make up everything around us. Atoms are composed of protons, neutrons, and electrons.

BACTERIA
Tiny single-celled organisms that make up one of the main types of life on Earth.

BAROMETER
An instrument that measures air pressure.

BASE
A substance with a pH value of more than 7.

BIG BANG
A scientific theory that explains how the Universe began around 13.8 billion years ago.

BIOLOGY
The scientific study of living things.

CELL
The smallest unit of a living thing. Cells are the building blocks of all living things.

CHEMICAL
Another word for a substance – usually one made up of several elements.

CHEMICAL REACTION
A process in which the atoms of one or more substances are rearranged, causing a new substance to be formed.

CHEMISTRY
The scientific study of substances, and what causes them to change.

COMPOUND
A substance made up of two or more elements.

CONDUCTOR
A substance through which heat or electricity flows easily.

CURRENT
The flow of an electric charge.

DNA
A chemical called deoxyribonucleic acid, which stores genetic information inside a cell.

EARTH SCIENCE
The scientific study of Earth, and the air around it.

ELECTRICITY
The flow of energy caused by the movement of electrons.

ELECTRON
One of the three main particles in an atom. Electrons orbit the atom's nucleus. They carry a negative charge.

ELEMENT
A pure substance that cannot be broken down into a simpler substance.

ENERGY
A force that makes things happen.

EON
The longest period of geologic time (the period of time it has taken Earth's rocks to form).

EQUATOR
The imaginary circle that divides Earth into equal northern and southern hemispheres.

ERA
A long period of geologic time. Two or more eras make up an eon.

ESCAPE VELOCITY
The speed at which an object needs to travel to escape Earth's gravity and fly into space.

EVOLUTION
The gradual change of a living thing as it adapts to its environment by natural selection.

FORCE
A push or pull on an object. Forces can make an object change speed, direction, or shape.

FOSSIL
The preserved remains or traces of organisms that have set into rock.

GALAXY
A large collection of stars and clouds of gas and dust held together by gravity. There are billions of galaxies in the Universe.

GAS
A substance that can take any shape or fill any container. In gases, particles move around freely.

GENE
The bits of information inside a living thing's cells that are passed down from parents to their offspring and affect its characteristics.

GENETICS
The study of how genes are passed on from parents to offspring.

GEOLOGY
The study of rocks and minerals.

GLOBAL POSITIONING SYSTEM
A system of satellites on Earth and in space that helps us know where we are and how to get to where we want to go.

GLOBAL WARMING
A rise in Earth's average temperature caused by human activity.

GRAVITY
An invisible force that pulls things together. It keeps our feet on the ground and makes objects fall to Earth when dropped.

GRAVITY ASSIST
The use of a planet's gravitational force by a spacecraft as it flies past to help change its speed.

HYGROMETER
An instrument that measures the air's humidity.

LATITUDE
A measure of how far north or south of the equator you are.

LIGHT
A form of energy that allows us to see.

LIGHT-YEAR
The distance light travels in one year, used as a measurement to describe distances in space.

LIQUID
A substance that flows easily and changes shape to fill the space around it. Particles in liquids move around freely.

LONGITUDE
A measure of how far east or west you are. It is measured from the Prime Meridian, an imaginary line from the North Pole to the South Pole that runs through Greenwich, London, UK.

MAGNET
An object that pulls certain types of metal to itself, creating a force called a magnetic field.

MASS
The amount of matter in an object, measured in kilograms, grams, or tonnes.

MATTER
The stuff that makes up everything around us.

METAL
One of a group of elements that share very useful properties, such as being strong, easy to shape, and able to conduct electricity.

MICROBES
Tiny organisms, such as bacteria and viruses, that can only be seen using a microscope. Some microbes are harmful to living things.

MILKY WAY
A massive galaxy of billions of stars, shaped like a spiral. The Sun and the planets of our Solar System all lie within the Milky Way.

MINERAL
A naturally occurring substance found in rocks.

MOLECULE
Two or more atoms joined together.

NATURAL SELECTION
The process by which living things adapt over a long period of time to changes in their environment in order to survive.

NEUTRON
One of the two main particles in the nucleus of an atom. Neutrons have no electric charge.

NUCLEAR
Relating to the nucleus of an atom. Nuclear energy is created when the nucleus is broken apart or when two nuclei are fused together.

NUCLEUS
In physics, the nucleus is the central part of an atom, made up of protons and neutrons. In biology, it is the control centre of a living thing's cell, where all its DNA is stored.

ORGANISM
A living thing.

OZONE
A type of oxygen that forms a layer of Earth's atmosphere. It protects us from the Sun's rays.

PARTICLE
A tiny portion of matter, such as an atom or a molecule.

PERIODIC TABLE
A table that identifies all the known elements.

PH SCALE
A scale used to measure how acidic or basic a substance is.

PHYSICS
The scientific study of how the Universe works, dealing with subjects such as energy, motion, space, and time.

POLYMER
A very large molecule formed of lots of smaller molecules joined together in chains. Many have useful properties, such as being strong.

PRESSURE
The amount of force that is acting on an area.

PROTON
One of the two main particles in the nucleus of an atom. Protons carry a positive charge.

RADIATION
The transfer of energy in the form of waves or particles from one place to another.

RADIOACTIVE
While most atoms are stable, meaning they don't change over time, some atoms are unstable, which means they can be broken down to release radiation. We call these unstable atoms radioactive.

SCIENTIFIC METHOD
The way in which scientists discover new facts by testing ideas with experiments.

SOLAR SYSTEM
The Sun and all the objects that orbit around it, including Earth and all the other planets. It is a very small part of the Milky Way.

SOLID
A substance that has a fixed shape. In solids, the particles are tightly bound to each other.

SOLUTION
A mixture in which the molecules of a substance are spread out in a liquid.

SONAR
A way of detecting objects by sending out sound waves and interpreting their echoes.

STAR
A giant ball of very hot gas, mainly hydrogen and helium, held together by gravity.

STATIC ELECTRICITY
A build-up of electric charge on the surface of an object causes static (non-moving) electricity.

THERMOMETER
A device used to measure temperature.

UNIVERSE
The whole of space, and everything it contains.

VIRUS
A tiny parasite that infects living cells and makes them manufacture copies of itself.

X-RAY
A type of radiation that can be used to take pictures inside the body.

INDEX

ACKNOWLEDGMENTS

DK would like to thank the following people for their assistance in the preparation of this book:

Editorial Assistant: Zaina Budaly; Additional Writing: Maliha Abidi; Picture Research: Vagisha Pushp; Picture Research Manager: Taiyaba Khatoon; Cutouts and Retouches: Neeraj Bhatia; Jacket Designer: Juhi Sheth; DTP Designer: Rakesh Kumar; Jackets Editorial Coordinator: Priyanka Sharma; Managing Jackets Editor: Saloni Singh; Index: Helen Peters; Proofreading: Victoria Pyke.

The publisher would like to thank the following for their kind permission to reproduce their photographs:

(Key: a-above; b-below/bottom; c-center; f-far; l-left; r-right; t-top)

10 Shutterstock.com: gillmar (crb). 14 Getty Images: Barcroft Media / Feature China (cb). 19 Dreamstime.com: Sdecoret (cra). 23 123RF.com: angellodeco (cra). 27 Science Photo Library: Michael J Daly (cra). 31 Dreamstime.com: Photka (br). 35 Alamy Stock Photo: Minden Pictures / Buiten-beeld / Otto Plantema (br). 46 Getty Images / iStock: PARETO (br). 50 Alamy Stock Photo: Dino Fracchia (clb); Science Photo Library / Alfred Pasieka (crb). Science Photo Library: Biografx / Kenneth Eward (cb). 51 Depositphotos Inc: NASA.image (cra). 55 Dreamstime. com: Monkey Business Images (br). 62 Shutterstock.com: Shin Okamoto (crb). 67 Dreamstime.com: Imtmphoto (br). 70 Dreamstime.com: Paul Reid (cr). 75 Dreamstime.com: South12th (bc). 79 Alamy Stock Photo: SWNS (cr). 83 Alamy Stock Photo: Cultura Creative RF / Monty Rakusen (cra). 94 Alamy Stock Photo: John Bentley (tr). 97 Dorling Kindersley: Science Museum, London / Dave King (br). 98 Alamy Stock Photo: Maria Galan Clik (bc). 103 Dreamstime.com: Seadam (bc). 115 Alamy Stock Photo: Naeblys (bc). 117 Alamy Stock Photo: Science History Images / Photo Researchers (crb). 118 Alamy Stock Photo: Science History Images / Photo Researchers (tr)

All other images © Dorling Kindersley

For further information, see: www.dkimages.com